Leader Guide

Partners in Learning

a
family
confirmation
approach

Contributors:

**Jeffrey Kunze, Gregory Sawyer, Wayne Schroeder,
Roger Sonnenberg, Timothy Wesemann**

Consultant: Dr. John Oberdeck

Contibutors:

Rev. Jeffrey Kunze is associate pastor of Immanuel Lutheran Church, St. Charles, MO, and has a background in theater.

Rev. Gregory Sawyer is associate pastor of Faith Lutheran Church, Grand Blanc, MI, holds a Ph.D. in counseling, and has extensive experience in educational youth ministry.

Rev. Wayne Schroeder is executive for congregational services for the South Wisconsin District of the LCMS. He developed the family approach to confirmation while pastor at Trinity Lutheran, Cedar Rapids, IA.

Rev. Roger Sonnenberg is senior pastor of Our Savior Lutheran Church, Arcadia, CA, second vice-president of the Pacific Southwest District of the LCMS, and a noted speaker on family ministry.

Rev. Timothy Wesemann is known for his devotional writing and children's curricula with Lutheran Hour Ministries and Concordia Publishing House. He is a freelance writer and lives in St. Louis, MO.

Consultant:

Rev. Dr. John Oberdeck is assistant professor of practical theology and director of continuing education and parish services for Concordia Seminary, St. Louis, MO. He holds a Ph.D. in education from the University of Missouri.

Edited by Edward Engelbrecht and Rodney Rathmann

This publication is available in braille and in large print for the visually impaired. Write to the Library for the Blind, 1333 S. Kirkwood Rd., St. Louis, MO 63122-7295; or call 1-800-433-3954.

All Scripture quotations are from the HOLY BIBLE, NEW INTERNATIONAL VERSION®. NIV®. Copyright © 1973, 1978, 1984 by International Bible Society. Used by permission of Zondervan Publishing House. All rights reserved.

Mission stories for the "Table Talk" sections in lessons 20, 21, and 25 are used by permission of LCMS World Mission.

Copyright © 2001 Concordia Publishing House
3558 S. Jefferson Avenue, St. Louis, MO 63118-3968
Manufactured in the United States of America

1   2   3   4   5   6   7   8   9   10   10   09   08   07   06   05   04   03   02   01

Contents

Why Use *Partners in Learning?*

"Thanks for coming in for the parents' confirmation conference. We have an exciting year of learning ahead of us!"

"Pastor, I'm concerned about the schedule you sent. Nancy has some volleyball games that conflict with the catechism classes. And, once again, there's too much memory work."

"And will they wear robes for confirmation service this year? The white ones they used last year didn't look good at all."

"Thanks for your interest. I have a lot to share with you about schedules, activities, and even robes. But before we get into all that, I want you to share something with me. Think back for a moment to the day Nancy was born and when you brought her home from the hospital. Describe what it was like for you to be entrusted by God with a new life ..."

As you prepare for this year's catechism classes, take time to meet with the parents and make them your partners in learning. Dr. Martin Luther had parents in mind when he prepared the catechism. At the introduction to each part, Luther wrote that "the head of the family should teach it in a simple way to his household." But parental instruction isn't just Luther's opinion. God desires that your students learn the faith from their parents (Deuteronomy 6:4–9).

When parents cannot or will not participate in class as catechists, ask them who could serve as a mentor. (Consider grandparents, godparents, other family members, or mature members of your congregation.) Parental or mentor involvement builds your students into the life of the congregation. It creates relationships with mature Christians that your confirmands can turn to when they need encouragement. If you cannot arrange for par-

Three Ways to Use *Partners in Learning*

	One-on-One	**Small Group**	**Traditional**
Serves	Any class size	Larger classes, divided into small groups	Any class size
Requires	Teacher and mentors (preferably parents)	Teacher and one mentor per student group	Only a teacher
Advantage	Relationship building between mentor and student	Relationship building between students	Relationship building between teacher and students
Challenge	Finding enough mentors	Guiding discussion	Limited personal application

ent or mentor participation for every student, do not become discouraged! Form small groups around the parents/mentors who do volunteer. *Partners in Learning* will work well in the small-group format. Or use *Partners in Learning* as the basis for your traditional confirmation classes and begin educating your students—who will be the parents of future confirmands—about their calling as Christian parents. The chart on page 4 will help you compare the different classroom models.

How Is *Partners in Learning* Different?

Many catechism classes try to involve parents by sending home "family time" activities or by encouraging parents to talk to their children about their catechism studies. In reality, many families fail to follow through. By bringing parents/mentors and students together for each class session, family confirmation instruction enables parents and children to
- learn (and review) the basic doctrines of the Christian faith as presented in Luther's Small Catechism.
- share their faith in Jesus Christ with one another.
- assess their value system based on God's Word.
- develop a better relationship with one another, centered in Jesus Christ.
- learn together about congregational life.
- model Christian devotion.
- undertake acts of service and mission together.

To understand *Partners in Learning* and use it most effectively in your catechism classes, please take a few moments to read about the design and components of the lessons. As you read, remember that no one knows your confirmation class better than you. Prayerfully consider how you can adapt the lessons to best meet your students' needs.

Applying the Lessons

Variety and Learning

Though some education philosophers insist on following a particular method for learning, most research shows that students learn in different ways. For example, some students perk up at reading time, others crave group activities, and still others are excellent listeners. *Partners in Learning* uses a variety of learning approaches to help maintain interest and to reach each student.

Focus on the Catechism

Too often confirmation classes end up serving a purpose other than teaching the Small Catechism as a summary of biblical faith and devotion. For example, some classes turn into a mini-dogmatics course, attempting to cover every point of Christian doctrine and ethics. Other classes become an excuse for community building. *Partners in Learning* endeavors to avoid such extremes by focusing on the teachings and devotions in the Small Catechism. Each class begins and ends with the words of the catechism. Each exercise or activity ties in with the catechism.

Teens Are in Transition

The changes your students experience at this time of life present special challenges to you as a teacher of the faith. One moment a student may be as serious as a congregational elder. Soon afterward you'd think the same student had transformed into a kindergartner! Your students aren't crazy; they're simply struggling in the transition between childhood and adulthood.

The exercises in *Partners in Learning* are designed for teens in transition. The dramas and activities will appeal to their nervous energy and need to cut up. The prayers and true-life stories will model Christian maturity. Mentoring, reflection, and group activities will help build lasting relationships that guide your students through the troublesome teen years and prepare them for congregational life.

Lesson Components

Opening and Closing Prayers

When Luther wrote the Small Catechism, he had no intention of creating a textbook. For example, the earliest version of the catechism was a prayer book (the *Little Prayer Book*, published in 1522). The opening and closing prayers in *Partners in Learning* build on this understanding of the catechism as a prayer/devotion. To reinforce this idea for your students, have them rise for prayer (just as they would in church) and pray the catechism responsively. For example,

Leader: The First Commandment

Students: You shall have no other gods.

Leader: What does this mean?

Students: We should fear, love, and trust in God above all things.

Leader: Lord, there's no one else like You …

Students: Amen.

Remember, you are not just teaching the students about doctrine, but shaping and modeling adult Christian life in the congregation of believers.

Focus Activity

Most likely, you will teach your catechism classes on weeknights after school or on a Saturday morning. This means your students will enter the classroom tired from hours at school or drowsy from just getting out of bed. To brighten the students' eyes and prepare them for learning, use the focus activity.

During His earthly ministry, Jesus frequently taught the truths of heaven through earthly activities or objects (e.g., Matthew 16:2–4; 17:24–27; 18:1–4; 22:15–22). *Partners in Learning* takes a similar approach in its focus activities. Expect a certain amount of commotion during the activities as students interact with one another and build working relationships. Enlist the help of parents/mentors in gathering materials (see the supplies list on page 12).

Table Talk

Despite our technological advances, the primary means of communicating God's Word remains the "foolishness" of preaching (1 Corinthians 1:21). To prepare for adult congregational life, your students must learn how to listen to a sermon. Practice telling the true-life stories of Table Talk just as you would practice delivering a sermon. Have the students listen and prepare to answer the discussion questions. If the students are easily distracted, ask them to take notes or to close their eyes and focus on the story.

Each true-life story provides an example of how the teachings of God's Word—summarized in the catechism—connect with Christian life. The discussion questions will help the students understand the Law and Gospel applications of what they hear. Students should work through these questions with their parents/mentors.

Also note that in the first 12 lessons the Law is the primary subject. As suggested by C. F. W. Walther in *The Proper Distinction between Law and Gospel* (CPH, 1986), "When explaining the Law, do not mingle Gospel elements with your catechization, except in the conclusion" (p. 83). Students need to feel the full weight of the Law so that they recognize their inability to keep it. Then they will see how sorely they need the Gospel.

Bible Study

The Bible studies in *Partners in Learning* illustrate each portion of the catechism. Each student should have a Bible and take a turn reading from it. However, be sensitive to students with poor reading skills. Parents/mentors should guide the students through the worksheet and direct them toward the correct answers provided on the reproducible pages of this Leader Guide. *Partners in Learning* assumes that your students will attend Divine Services and Sunday school. Therefore, these Bible studies are not intended to provide students with a comprehensive knowledge of Bible history. They focus on teaching the catechism. Teachers who wish to present further insights from *LSCE* or another source should consider offering them either at the opening or the close of the Bible Study.

Family in Faith Journal

As students and parents/mentors read God's Word and pray together, something marvelous happens: they grow in admiration for one another as fellow believers. The Family in Faith Journal provides an opportunity to capture that experience and create a lifelong keepsake. Students and their parents/mentors should take turns writing in the journal as instructed in the lessons. Students should also be encouraged to journal thoughts and prayers, add photographs, or even doodle. Families may wish to purchase a quality journal or use a sturdy composition notebook.

"Fun for Review" Dramas

In the German Bible translations of 1534 and 1545, Luther compares the book of Judith to a play and commends the use of both comic and tragic dramas for teaching the "folk" and the young (*Weimar Ausgabe, Deutsche Bibel*, vol. 12, p. 109). *Partners in Learning* includes dramas for just this purpose.

By the time students have worked through the study questions, they will be ready for something more active. The dramas provide students with an opportunity to review the main points of the lessons in an active way. If you have a large class, assign the dramas to different groups on a rotating basis. In smaller groups, use a readers' theater approach. To make sure the students get the point of the drama, follow up with the discussion questions.

Lesson Suggestions

At the end of each lesson in the Leader Guide, you will find suggestions for music (from *Lutheran Worship*, *The Lutheran Hymnal*, and *All God's People Sing*), homework assignments (with references to *Exploring Luther's Small Catechism*), and memory work. Feel free to tailor each lesson to the particular needs or interests of your students.

Classroom Setting

Partners in Learning assumes that students and their parents or mentors will sit together. If possible, arrange tables so that one or two families are seated per table and can see the front of the room. Round tables work best for small-group interaction. In large classes you may want to use individual "table cards" (one with each confirmand's name on it) so that participants can be moved from week to week. That way different families can interact with each other.

Before You Confirm

Lutheran churches have traditionally based confirmation on three Bible passages. Review these passages and prayerfully consider your students' maturity in the faith.

Matthew 28:19–20
- I am baptized in the name of the triune God.
- I have learned God's Word as summarized by the Ten Commandments, the Apostles' Creed, and the Lord's Prayer.
- I believe these teachings by the grace of God's Holy Spirit, and by His power I strive to obey them.

Matthew 10:32–33
- I publicly confess that Jesus Christ has saved me from sin by His death and resurrection.
- I actively participate in Divine Services.
- I can witness about salvation in Christ to those outside the church.

1 Corinthians 11:28
- I examine my life and faith before coming to the Lord's Supper.

Note: The letter on pages 10–11, "Mentoring Made Easy," may be reproduced and distributed to parents and other potential mentors of your students.

Mentoring Made Easy
(or at least easier!)

Mentoring—an intimidating term. But before you say no to serving as a mentor, consider this: more than likely, you've mentored someone before. To help you understand what mentoring is and how it works in *Partners in Learning*, read the following examples.

Assistant Coach

When young people commit to a team, they always need help understanding how the game is played. They need the counsel and example of someone who's been around the game before. An assistant coach doesn't have to be a genius. All he needs to do is offer a little assistance, help run the drills, and speak a word of encouragement.

If you've ever helped out as an assistant coach or played ball with your kids in the backyard, you already have experience as a mentor. Sure, there's always more to learn. But don't count yourself out because you've never tried it before!

Den Mother

Moms who help out when their children join the Boy Scouts or Girl Scouts are rarely expert woodsmen. But by going over the directions, assisting with a craft, or telling someone, "Well done!," they play the role of a mentor. It's that simple.

Baptismal Sponsor

When someone is baptized at church, one or more volunteers stand beside him or her to offer support and encouragement. These sponsors pledge to help the newly baptized person live out his or her faith and grow in knowledge and service.

When you become a mentor, you are simply living out the vows that Christians make when someone is baptized. No miracles will be required of you—just prayerful, caring service for those who are young in Christ.

Millennial Children

As parents or mentors, we must pay special attention to the children we mentor. Children today are known as the "Millennial Generation." The first Mills were born around 1982 and began graduating from high school in 2000. They differ from the Boomers and Generation X in significant ways.
- Millennials were planned and wanted by their parents. To some extent they've been overindulged, pampered, and even spoiled, never experiencing a serious downturn in the economy.
- The society that surrounds Millennials has rediscovered children. Things

like school violence make their parents grow more protective and less tolerant of deviant behavior.

- Millennials feel less of a generation gap and are more open to institutions like the church. They hold the promise of being the next great generation of philanthropists. They don't seem to mind uniforms and like being part of groups.
- Millenials are open to spiritual matters and seem to favor tradition, ritual, and liturgy. They find order in these things amidst lives filled with change and even chaos. They are visually oriented and love stories.
- Millennials are growing up in a world that recognizes no absolute truth, where each person defines his or her own faith and value system. They may challenge the church as it shares *the* truth of God's Word.
- Millennials live in a wired world and have access to all the world's knowledge—good and bad—via the Internet (earning them the nickname "fingertip children").
- The best way to reach Millennials is relationally, interactively, and experientially. Engage them in the learning experience.

Because of changes in our society and changes in schools, teaching millennial children may require more creative approaches than we have used for confirmation in the past. Instead of just teaching the truths of the catechism, we will need to help students experience why such truths are important. We will have to tell more of our stories and share some of the consequences we've experienced in life. We must nurture them with events that teach God's truth and help them understand God's purpose in life and death. As millennial children get to know adults who love Jesus, they will grow in their love for Jesus too. *Partners in Learning* is designed with millenial children in mind.

Involvement

Don't let these observations discourage you. Young people of every generation naturally look to their elders for guidance. Remember, they're experiencing these things for the first time. They *need* your guidance. Patiently share with them God's Word and your life experiences as a child of God. The Holy Spirit will bless you and your teaching according to Christ's promise!

As mentors, you will sit with students in class and guide them through the Bible study worksheet. You don't have to be a Bible scholar. The Leader Guide for *Partners in Learning* contains reproducible answer sheets to make your job easier. You will also work with your student to journal life experiences in the Family in Faith Journal. Feel free to help with the learning activities, dramas, and service events. The bottom line: You will simply serve as a partner in the learning process!

Supplies List for
Partners in Learning Activities and Dramas

Lesson 1: Note cards, magnets, paper clips, tape

Lesson 2: One toothbrush per student, small cup filled with cleaning powder for each student, cup of water for each student, paper towels, toothpaste

Lesson 3: Dominos, poster putty

Lesson 4: Long rope

Lesson 5: Old newsmagazines or newspapers, scissors, glue, 2 sheets of poster board, newspaper for skit

Lesson 6: Pipe cleaners—one per student, wire cutters

Lesson 7: Various types and sizes of shoes—some too small for class members and some too large

Lesson 8: Advertisement clippings, tape, dartboard, darts

Lesson 9: Balloons, pins, tape

Lesson 10: 2 buckets, variety of weighty items, set of weights labeled "Thanks," pirate's patches, paper and pen/pencil

Lesson 11: 3 to 5 belts, 3 chairs

Lesson 12: Red construction paper, black markers, scissors, safety pins, phone (if available)

Lesson 13: Flower or vegetable seeds, pot, potting soil, fertilizer, water

Lesson 14: Candle and candleholder, matches, oscillating fan, plastic bottle, sunglasses (if available)

Lesson 15: Iron, squirt bottle filled with water, chairs, cushion or pillow

Lesson 16: None

Lesson 17: Freshly popped corn, sign reading "LAW," sign reading "GOSPEL," sign reading "Right Path," sign reading "Wrong Path"

Lesson 18: None

Lesson 19: Copies of the Ten Commandments

Lesson 20: Cell phone and pager, play food and cooking utensils, apron, chef's hat (if available), trays and napkins—items a waiter may use

Lesson 21: Sign with "Walk" printed on it, sign with "Stop" printed on it, 2 chairs

Lesson 22: Overhead or slide projector, transparency or picture of tablets of the Ten Commandments, Kleenex

Lesson 23: Lamp, 2 light bulbs (one working and one burned out)

Lesson 24: Sheet of paper with "Blessings and Thanksgiving" written in very small print, binoculars, tape, board, markers, paper sack

Lesson 25: Suitcase filled with books to make it as heavy as possible, 2 pretend microphones

Lesson 26: Vacuum with an attachment and hose, paper (that can be sucked up to the end of the attachment and held in place), markers, large rock with "The Word" written on it

Lesson 27: None

Lesson 28: Several packages of instant pudding, milk to prepare pudding, hand mixer or whisk, notebook

Lesson 29: Pair of clean white socks, pair of very dirty white socks, Bible

Lesson 30: 6 to 10 belts to bind 2 students together

Lesson 31: Vinegar, baking soda, 2 containers with snap-on lids, yardstick

Lesson 32: Small suitcase with a working lock and key, filled with enough candy for all students; several keys strung together

Lesson 33: Pre-measured ingredients for chocolate chip cookies, spoons, Bible, notebook paper and pencil, notepad and pen, calculator

Lesson 34: Variety of food and beverage items, Communion chalice and wafers

Lesson 35: Warm coat, gloves, rope, sleeping bag, backpack, other hiking or mountain gear that is easily accessible

Introduction and Prayer for the Catechumens

Following the sermon, the confirmands and their parents/mentors shall come forward. They shall face the congregation, confirmands in front and parents/mentors behind. Then the minister shall say:

Beloved in the Lord, our Lord Jesus Christ said: "All authority in heaven and on earth has been given to Me. Therefore go and make disciples of all nations, baptizing them in the name of the Father and of the Son and of the Holy Spirit and teaching them to obey everything I have commanded you. And surely I will be with you always, to the very end of the age."

Likewise, our Lord said: "Whoever confesses Me before men, I will also confess him before My Father in heaven. But he that denies Me before men, I will deny him before My Father in heaven."

And the apostle Paul wrote: "A man ought to examine himself before he eats of the bread and drinks of the cup. For anyone who eats and drinks without recognizing the body of the Lord eats and drinks judgment on himself."

Each student shall introduce himself/herself by name.

These students will soon begin a careful study of God's Word as summarized in Luther's Small Catechism, preparing to confess Christ publicly and grow with us in faith and service. Therefore, let us pray for our catechumens, that our Lord God would open their hearts and the door of His mercy that they may remain faithful to Christ Jesus, our Lord:

Almighty God and Father, because You always grant growth to Your church, increase the faith and understanding of our catechumens that, recalling the new birth by the water of Holy Baptism, they may forever continue in the family of those whom You adopt as Your sons and daughters; through Jesus Christ, our Lord.

Response: Amen.

Adapted from *Lutheran Worship*, pp. 205, 276.

First Commandment

Focus on the Catechism

Focus the attention of the group by reciting the First Commandment responsively (*Luther's Small Catechism with Explanation,* p. 9; see p. 7 of this Leader Guide for an example of how to pray the catechism responsively). Then pray this or a similar prayer based on the commandment:

Lord, there's no one else like You. You surprise us with your awesome power. You love us above all things in Your creation. You entrust us with the gift of life itself. As we study Your Word today, teach us to fear, love, and trust in You above all things, for You, O Father, Son, and Holy Spirit, live and reign, one God, now and forever. Amen.

Activity

Materials: Note cards, magnets, paper clips, tape

Using note cards, have students list three things that are most important to them. Give a refrigerator magnet and a paper clip to the students (the magnet should not be too strong; experiment with it before class). Show them how the two cling to each other. Then have the students slip one of their cards in between the paper clip and the magnet. The paper clip should no longer cling to the magnet or only cling loosely. Say, **If something comes between the magnet and the paper clip, they will not hold together. Just as the magnet draws the metal to itself, God draws us to Himself. But if we permit anything in our lives—even important things—to come between God and us, then God is not number one in our lives. We do not fear, love, and trust in God above all things.**

Have students use a piece of tape to attach the card to the bottom of the paper clip. Now lift both the paper clip and the card by touching the magnet to the paper clip. Say, **In the First Commandment God is not commanding you to give up everything else in your life. He created everything for you. Instead, the First Commandment means that no thing or person should ever come between you and your God. That's why God sent His Son, Jesus: to draw you to Himself (John 12:32).**

Ask, **Is there anything or anyone in your life today that has come between you and God? Have you made someone or something else a god in your life?**

Table Talk

(Don't just read—TELL the following true story.)

John Bernardone was the son of a wealthy cloth merchant in Italy. He received an excellent education, surrounded himself with friends, and *enjoyed* his family's wealth. When John was 20 years old and anxious for adventure, he joined a military expedition with his friends. But the enemy captured him and he spent a year in prison.

While John was in prison, God changed him. Although John returned home to a full wallet, excellent food, and the best clothes, he could not return to his previous way of life. Instead of living for himself, he devoted his life to serving Jesus and helping the poor. John gave up the family business and everything else that came between him and His Savior. Today we know him as St. Francis.

Discuss one-on-one or in small groups the following questions. (Mentors will guide students through the lesson sheets.)

➡ Student material starts here.

Did St. Francis have to give up his family's business in order to keep the First Commandment? As a cloth merchant, how might he have used his family's business to fear, love, and trust in God?

No. He could have used his family's business to help clothe people.

Would anyone like to share an example of something or someone that might interfere with your relationship with God?

Answers will vary.

How might keeping the First Commandment change your relationship with your family, friends, and others?

Students will follow God's Word before following the advice of other people.

Bible Study

God defeats the Egyptians and frees the children of Israel from slavery. Through Moses, God leads the Israelites to Mount Sinai. Read Exodus 19:17–20:3.

1. What fearful things did Moses and the people of Israel experience when God drew near to Mount Sinai?

Eyes saw: *Smoke, fire*
Ears heard: *Trumpet*
Nose smelled: *Smoke*
Body felt: *Trembling*

2. Before commanding the Israelites to "have no other gods," how did the Lord remind them of His love? See Exodus 20:2.

He declared that He was their God. He led them out of Egypt.

3. Imagine that you stand at the foot of Mount Sinai, seeing and hearing the fearful things you described in question 1. What words in this story would lead you to trust God above all things?

The words in Exodus 20:2 show God's care for His people in the past.

4. Read Luke 23:39–43. Contrast what happened at Mount Sinai with what happened with God's Son, Jesus, at Mount Calvary. Why could the thief trust Jesus? See also Luke 23:34.

At Sinai, God's presence was fearful. But on Calvary, God's Son suffered and died for our sins. The thief recognized that Jesus was innocent and forgiving.

5. Why did God give us the Law?

To show us right and wrong, but, most importantly, to show us that we are sinful and need a Savior.

6. The Law cannot save us. We cannot keep God's Law perfectly. But who has kept the Law perfectly for us and our salvation?

Jesus. He alone can save us.

7. How are we Christians able to fear, love, and trust in God above all things?

Only by the grace and power of Jesus' forgiveness and love imparted to us in and through the Gospel.

Family in Faith Journal

Brainstorm with the students three ways to keep God number one in their lives. Have students record them in the Family in Faith Journal.

Fun for Review

Characters: Announcer, three "Team Shellfish" members (TS1, TS2, TS3), three "Team One.com" members (TOC1, TOC2, TOC3)

Setting: ANNOUNCER stands in the front of class. TEAM SHELLFISH is on one side, TEAM ONE.COM on the other.

ANNOUNCER: Ladies and gentlemen, welcome to tonight's main event. Let's get ready to ruum-mmmble! Now give it up for our first group, "Team Shellfish"!

(Players enter to applause.)

TS: *(Chanting together)* We're number one! We're number one! We're number one!

ANNOUNCER: *(To TS1)* It looks like your team is ready and pumped.

TS1: We're the best! We're number one! We're rockin' tonight and every night.

TS2: We have the biggest muscles, the fastest legs, the strongest arms …

TS3: We have the quickest reactions and make the fastest decisions. Without a doubt, we're number one.

TS: *(Chanting together)* We're number one! We're number one! We're number one!

ANNOUNCER: Let's meet the other group now, "Team One-dot-Com"!

(Players enter to applause.)

TOC: *(Chanting together)* You're number one! You're number one!

TS1: What are you fools saying?

TOC1: You're number one! You're number one!

TS3: What are you talking about? You're supposed to say, "We're number one!" not "You're number one!"

TOC1: But I'm not number one.

TS2: What has happened to your sense of self-esteem?

TS1: You're supposed to watch out for numero uno!

TS3: What pushovers! They're even admitting that we're number one.

TOC2: We're not saying that **you're** number one.

TS2: We're not deaf and dumb. You just said, "You're number one!" You are saying that we're number one.

TOC3: No, no, no! We're talking about the meaning of our team's name. The name of our team and our cheer remind us of what is really important—no matter what we are doing.

TOC2: One-dot-com. First Commandment. God is above all things. Get it?

TS1: Who cares? Your team is lame.

TOC1: When we say, "You're number one," we're talking to God. He's number one; we're not.

TOC3: We know that we wouldn't be able to compete tonight without Him.

TOC2: We wouldn't have legs or arms, brains or skills, eyes or ears, time or effort without Him. He's number one.

TOC3: That helps put things in the proper perspective. He's number one in everything.

TOC1: It helps us from becoming shellfish, I mean, selfish.

TOC2: And what's really great is that no matter what happens when we use our body, mind, or talents, we know the victory is ours because … *(pointing upwards)* You're number one! You're number one!

TS1: I hate to admit it, but they have a great point. I say let's go for the victory. And since we can't beat 'em, let's join 'em.

ALL: *(Chanting together, pointing and looking upwards)* You're number one! You're number one! You're number one!

Finish the Lesson

What truth about the First Commandment did Team One.com illustrate? That we should fear, love, and trust in God above all things.

What reason did Team One.com give for saying that God is number one? He created everything, giving us all our strength and powers.

Closing Prayer

Focus the attention of the group by reciting the First Commandment responsively (*LSCE*, p. 9). Then pray this prayer or a similar prayer based on the First Commandment:

Lord, there's no one else like You. You surprise us with your awesome power. You love us above all things in Your creation. You entrust us with the gift of life itself. As we study Your Word today, teach us to fear, love, and trust in You above all things. Please forgive us when we fail; through Jesus Christ, our Lord. Amen.

Lesson Suggestions

Hymn: *LW* 331:1–2, 11–12; *TLH* 287; *AGPS* 165

Homework: *LSCE* questions 13–23. Have students write a summary paragraph of what they learned or answer the questions in *Exploring Luther's Small Catechism*, pages 8–9.

Memory Work: First Commandment; Deuteronomy 6:4 (45); 1 John 1:8 (75)

2 Second and Third Commandments

Focus on the Catechism

Focus the attention of the group by reciting the Second and Third Commandments responsively (*LSCE*, pp. 9–10). Then pray this or a similar prayer based on the Second and Third Commandments:

Lord, You command and invite us to use Your holy name in worship. As we learn Your commandments, help us to fear Your holiness so that we do not curse or swear by Your name. Stir us to love preaching and Your Word. May we now gladly hear and learn from You through Jesus Christ, our Lord. Amen.

Activity

Materials: One toothbrush per student, small cup filled with cleaning powder for each student, cup of water for each student, paper towels, toothpaste

Give each student a toothbrush, a cup filled with cleaning powder such as Ajax or Comet, and a cup of water. Ask students to clean either a spot on the floor, a part of a folding chair, or something else. Use paper towels to dry the spots where the students clean. Thank them for their effort and then ask each to come forward for a drop of toothpaste.

After the students have toothpaste on their brushes, ask them to brush their teeth. Listen to their reactions. Say, **What's wrong with using these toothbrushes for your teeth?** (It's disgusting to use a dirty toothbrush.) Say, **You have a specific purpose for your toothbrush. You probably do not use it to clean something and then brush your teeth. If someone used your toothbrush to clean the floor and then you put it in your mouth, how would you feel?**

Say, **These toothbrushes can remind us of how we should not use God's name.** Read Psalm 54:1 and 106:47 to learn the true use of His name.

The Second Commandment forbids us to misuse God's name by cursing or swearing. In contrast, the Third Commandment teaches us to worship by hearing God's Word and calling on God's name. When we use God's name for cursing or swearing instead of worship, we offend God.

Table Talk

(Don't just read—TELL the following true story.)

At the age of 17, Sebastian faced a crucial career choice. He could become a court musician and earn plenty of money, or he could become a church musician with an uncertain future. At that time, a popular movement called "Pietism" was sweeping through the churches. Pietists argued that God was not pleased with church music. They taught that God was more pleased when people prayed at home than when people gathered for church. Despite these pressures, young Sebastian determined to become a church musician, dedicating himself to writing church music to the glory of God.

During his lifetime, Sebastian wrote more than 300 songs (or cantatas), most of which were for singing at church. As he finished each song, he would sign not only his name but also write these three words: Soli Deo Gloria (Glory to God Alone). Today we know Sebastian as one of the most famous of all musicians—Johann Sebastian Bach.

Discuss one-on-one or in small groups the following questions. (Mentors will guide students through the lesson sheets.)

➡ Student material starts here.

How does the way Sebastian signed his music show that he understood the Second Commandment?

He glorified God's name.

What might the Pietists have learned by studying the Third Commandment?

God wants us to gather for the Divine Service.

How does Sebastian's career show that he understood the Third Commandment?

He dedicated himself to public worship.

Give some modern-day examples of how people in the media or at school misuse God's name.

Answers will vary.

How might keeping the Second and Third Commandments change your relationship with your family, friends, and others?

Answers will vary. For example, students wouldn't skip church.

Bible Study

When Moses is 80 years old, God calls him to lead the Israelites out of Egypt. In fear, Moses refuses to accept God's calling. But in response to each of Moses' objections, God gives His promises and His name. Read Exodus 3:1–15.

1. List Moses' objections in 3:11–14 and God's promises for each objection:

A. *"Who am I, that I should go to Pharaoh ... ?" (3:11); "I will be with you!" (3:12)*

B. *"Suppose . . . they ask me, 'What is His name?'" (3:13); "'I AM has sent me to you'" (3:14).*

2. What name does God use for Himself? See verse 14.

God identifies Himself as "I AM WHO I AM."

3. Our names distinguish us from other people. How does this special name for God distinguish Him from everyone else?

With the name "I AM," God declares Himself as unchangeable, as the eternally faithful God. He is from everlasting to everlasting. Why did that make the name even more special and more honored? His name identifies who He is. It defines Him as holy and deserving of our praise.

4. What comfort is there in knowing that God is "I AM"?

He is with us now and will be there for us always.

5. How should we reverence God's name that has such meaning for us?

We should desire to keep His name holy in our own lives. This means we should not misuse it in any way, but instead call upon it and give Him praise.

6. Moses did go and do what God had commanded and was blessed in his efforts. What blessings do we receive as we respond to God's command to worship each week?

Of ourselves, we do not deserve God's blessings. But through His Word and Sacraments, God gives us faith in His Son, Jesus, and strengthens us. He comforts and guides us (2 Timothy 3:16–17).

7. Ask your parent/mentor to explain why he/she appreciates worship.

Answers will vary.

8. The Law cannot save us. We cannot keep God's Law perfectly. But who has kept God's Law for us and our salvation?

Jesus. He alone can save us.

Family in Faith Journal

Briefly describe an example of giving a name to a child. If possible, look up the meaning of each student's name. Students should record these memories in the Family in Faith Journal.

Fun for Review

Characters: Narrator, Suzy, Amy, Bill, Bobby

Setting: Outside church after worship

NARRATOR: Okay, here's the scene: our wonderful group of eighth graders decides to worship together. What you're about to witness could happen on any given Sunday.

(Kids enter exchanging excited comments.)

GROUP: Wow! Cool! Yeah, that was great!

SUZY: What a cool sermon! *(High fives are exchanged.)* I can't wait to go back! Yeah!

NARRATOR: *(Frantic)* WAIT! Let's be a little more realistic, shall we? You're in eighth grade, remember?

(Kids back up, go in reverse, and once again enter—a little more solemn.)

AMY: *(Proper)* That was a nice sermon.

SUZY: *(Replying to AMY, but side-glance to NARRATOR)* Yeah. I still think it was *(pause for emphasis; more politely)* rather cool.

NARRATOR: Now Bill has something to share …

BILL: Hey! Did you guys hear about my aunt?

BOBBY: Is this another bug joke?

BILL: Um … no. No joke. She's very ill. My mom says she may not make it out of the hospital.

SUZY: No way!

AMY: Wow. Sorry, Bill.

SUZY: Yeah. Sorry, man.

BILL: Thanks. I wish I would have remembered to tell the pastor so we could have prayed for her in church. Now I guess I'll have to wait until next week.

BOBBY: Why don't you pray for her tonight … or, um … now?

BILL: I don't think my prayers will really count unless they're in church. Besides, I'm not really sure how I should pray for her. Aw, just forget it. Let's go.

AMY: That's ridiculous.

SUZY: Yeah. Out of touch.

BOBBY: You can call on the name of the Lord …

AMY: … anytime!

SUZY: … anywhere!

BOBBY: Don't you remember what the pastor said? "Call upon Me when there's trouble." You don't have to wait until Sunday. You can call on the Lord for help …

AMY: … anytime!

SUZY: … anywhere!

BOBBY: Even now I know God hears your prayers. And I know He likes it when we use His name not only on Sundays but …

(AMY and SUZY are both giggling.)

AMY: … anytime!

SUZY: … anywhere!

(They high five.)

BILL: Okay! I get the picture. I just hope He hears me and understands.

BOBBY: Yes. He hears you because we pray in the name of Jesus.

AMY: And He certainly understands.

SUZY: And He's, like, way in touch with what you need, man!

BOBBY: And remember, there's no other name you ever need to call upon in trouble or praise, but the name of our triune God.

NARRATOR: And so the kids continued on their way. Bill was comforted by the fact that he can call on the name of the Lord …

ALL STUDENTS: … anytime and anywhere!

Finish the Lesson

Brainstorm with the students some times or circumstances in their family life when they can stop and pray (e.g., when someone is ill, before a test). Assure the students that we can call on God's name at any time.

Closing Prayer

Focus the attention of the group by reciting the Second and Third Commandments responsively (*LSCE,* pp. 9–10). Then pray this prayer or a similar prayer based on these commandments:

Lord, You command and invite us to use Your holy name in worship. As we learn Your commandments, help us to fear Your holiness so that we do not curse or swear by Your name. Stir us to love preaching and Your Word. May we gladly hear and learn from You. Forgive us when we fail to call on Your name or gladly hear Your Word; through Jesus Christ, our Lord. Amen.

Lesson Suggestions

Hymn: *LW* 331:1, 3–4, 12; *TLH* 287; *AGPS* 267

Homework: *LSCE* questions 24–44. Have students write a summary paragraph of what they learned or answer the questions in *Exploring Luther's Small Catechism*, pages 10–13.

Memory Work: Second and Third Commandments

Fourth Commandment

Focus on the Catechism

Focus the attention of the group by reciting the Fourth Commandment responsively (*LSCE,* p. 10). Then pray this or a similar prayer based on the Fourth Commandment:

Lord, Your Word teaches that You are our Father and that You have given us life through our parents. Bind our families together in perfect love and honor. Teach us to love and cherish our parents and other authorities as blessings from You; through Jesus Christ, our Lord. Amen.

Activity

Materials: Dominos, poster putty

Divide the students into groups gathered around desks or tables. Give several dominos to each group. Ask the students to stand their dominos on end, forming some interesting pattern. Once each group has finished its construction project, test the stability of their dominos. Ask them to pound the desk gently or to knock over the first domino in the line. The dominos should fall easily.

Say, **These dominos show us how hard it is to stand alone. At this time in your life, many things are changing. Name some changes you and your friends experience right now.** Examples are their bodies, classes, and interests. **At times you may feel that life is shaking you up or knocking you down.**

Take three dominos and squeeze them together with a bit of poster putty between them. Stand them on a table and ask a student to pound the table gently. Say, **Remember how easily the dominos fell over with just a little shake or a push? Why are these dominos more stable?** They stay together—even when they fall. Say, **These dominos show us how parents and other adults bring strength and stability into our lives. In the Fourth Commandment, God tells us to love and cherish our parents and other caring adults as God's helpers.**

Table Talk

(Don't just read—TELL the following true story.)

To add light to his home in a sewer canal, 12-year-old Adrian lights a candle he stole from a nearby church. The candle illumines his bare arm, revealing a jagged nail scrape and a knife gash. He shivers, sniffles, and weeps in the cold air. But no one dries his tears. He lifts a filthy cloth, moistened with glue, and snuffs in the intoxicating fumes. For a moment he forgets the stronger children who steal his clothes and force him to beg in the streets.

According to a Knight Ridder news report, Adrian is one of 3,000 to 5,000 street children in the Romanian capital of Bucharest. Years ago, his parents abandoned him. Corruption and debt have so beset the Romanian government that it offers Adrian little help. The best the government can do is offer new parents $5.50 per month to keep their children at home rather than turn them loose in the streets like Adrian.

Discuss one-on-one or in small groups the following questions. (Mentors will guide students through the lesson sheets.)

➡ Student material starts here.

Contrast your life today with Adrian's. Why is your life so different?

Answers will vary. Adrian had no parents/guardians.

What might you tell a friend who is angry at his or her parents and thinking of running away from home?

You need your parents!

For the Fourth Commandment, who does Luther include in his definition of those in authority?

Luther includes all those placed over us at home, in government, at school, at the place where we work, and in the church.

Bible Study

Eli fails to raise his two sons in the way that they should go, and as a result both die prematurely. In contrast, Samuel heeds God's words and receives His blessings. Read 1 Samuel 2:12–36.

1. In what ways did Eli stretch God's patience too far in his service to God in the temple? See 1 Samuel 2:27–29.

Eli scorned God's sacrifice and offering and honored his sons more than he honored God.

2. Because Eli honored his wayward sons more than he honored God, there were some dire consequences. What were some of those consequences according to 1 Samuel 2:30–33? Read also 1 Samuel 4:10–11.

God cut short Eli's strength, and his household never saw any man grow old in the family line. His descendants died in the prime of life.

3. Consider the promise in 1 Samuel 2:35. This promise could not refer to Samuel. Its ultimate fulfillment was in someone far greater. Who was He? For help, see Hebrews 5:6.

Ultimately the faithful priest is Jesus, who fulfills all that the Old Testament priesthood signified.

4. Philippians 2:6–11 describes Jesus' obedience. What does His obedience on the cross mean to you and your family?

By obeying the Law, He took care of something we could not—to obey and fulfill the Law perfectly. Then He died on the cross so that we might have forgiveness and life eternal.

5. Name some consequences you've seen for children who have failed to "honor their parents."

Answers will vary.

6. Because of Jesus' "obedience to death" on the cross, what is the Good News for us as we consider our disobedience to Him and to our parents?

We have forgiveness for our disobedience.

7. Read Ephesians 6:1–3. What promise does God attach to the Fourth Commandment?

God makes it clear that He graciously blesses the obedience of His children according to His promise.

Family in Faith Journal

Have students describe for their parents/mentors a time when a parent gave them extra special help out of love (e.g., with homework, learning a sport). Also have parents/mentors briefly describe the enormity of God's love in Jesus. The parent/mentor should record these words in the Family in Faith Journal.

Fun for Review

Characters: Mom, Pops, Jon, Sue. Mom and Pops have Italian accents.

Setting: Bakery

MOM: Welcome to the famous Mom and Pop's Bakery.

JON: Thanks. My sister and I heard that you have the best rolls in town.

POPS: We specialize in parental "roles."

SUE: Excuse me? Did you say, "parental roles"?

POPS: I did.

SUE: Oh … maybe we came to the wrong place.

JON: Wait a minute, Sue. Let's see what they have.

MOM: Over in this case we have some great roles filled with respect.

POPS: Everyone in the family needs those.

SUE: That sounds good, but I don't know if they would go over in my house today.

MOM: Oh, but respect roles make everything else taste good.

POPS: It's impossible to yell and fight while you're chewing a respect role.

SUE: That's cool. *(Pointing)* What are those?

POPS: Those are our teen packs of obedience-filled roles.

JON: Aren't those hard to swallow?

MOM: Contrary to popular belief, they aren't at all.

POPS: Too many people don't even try them because they don't sound good.

SUE: They wouldn't be my first choice, but I hear they're good for you.

MOM: Sometimes people don't want things that are good for them! *(Looks at POPS. Both shake heads and say, "Agh!")*

JON: I'm guessing that those heart-shaped roles are love roles?

MOM: You'll never outgrow the taste for those.

Growing teenagers need them most.

POPS: That's for sure, Mama! Love never fails!

SUE: What about nutrients? Are all these roles healthful?

MOM: They make for the healthiest of relationships.

POPS: So many people hang out on the corner where they are swallowing angry, hateful, hurtful roles that can make people deadly sick. What they need are some good parental roles for a change!

JON: *(Pointing)* And this one over here looks like the best place to start—the forgiven role.

SUE: That's a great place to start. Wrap some forgiven roles to go.

JON: And box up some of those grace roles, please.

MOM: *(Boxing them up)* What else can we get you?

SUE: Mmmmm, some honor-filled roles. And how about serving up some service roles?

JON: Sue, I think we should just order a few of everything.

POPS: Now you're on a roll! Honey, get them at least one of everything!

MOM: You can stop by every day and pick up more. We never seem to run out.

SUE: We'll be back, that's for sure. And we'll tell our friends about you.

JON: By the way, I almost forgot why Mom and Dad sent us here—do you have any jelly rolls?

POPS: Jelly rolls? Hmmmm. Never thought of that!

MOM: No, we don't have any jelly rolls. Anyway, I can't imagine those catching on! I think we'll just stick with parental roles. They're the sensible food!

Finish the Lesson

Why are obedience-filled roles hard to swallow? Answers will vary. The most basic cause is the sin that corrupts us all.

What might make them go down easier? God's love and forgiveness in Christ change our hearts. God gives us His Holy Spirit so that we love His gifts, including our parents.

Closing Prayer

Focus the attention of the group by reciting the Fourth Commandment responsively (*LSCE*, p. 10). Then pray this or a similar prayer based on the Fourth Commandment:

Lord, Your Word teaches that You are our Father and that You have given us life through our parents. Bind our families together in perfect love and honor. Teach us to love and cherish our parents and other authorities as blessings from You. Please forgive us when we fail to respect our parents and other authorities; through Jesus Christ, our Lord. Amen.

Lesson Suggestions

Hymn: *LW* 331:1, 5, 11–12; *TLH* 287; *AGPS* 80

Homework: *LSCE* questions 45–51. Have students write a summary paragraph of what they learned or answer the questions in *Exploring Luther's Small Catechism*, pages 13–14.

Memory Work: Fourth Commandment; Ephesians 6:1–3 (see *LSCE*, p. 36)

4

Table of Duties, Church and State

Focus on the Catechism

Focus the attention of the group by reciting "What the Hearers Owe Their Pastors" and "Of Civil Government" responsively (*LSCE*, pp. 34–35). Then pray the following prayer based on the Table of Duties:

Lord, those who serve You in the church and state are Your gifts to Your people. Help us to show loving respect for those in authority and make their work a joy, not a burden; through Christ, our Lord. Amen.

Activity

Materials: Long rope

At times we want to make our own rules and disregard the rules of the authorities God has established. This can happen at home, school, the mall, or maybe even here at church. However, God has established a line of authority for our safety.

Ask for two volunteers. They will hold the ends of the rope. Now ask four more volunteers to hold other parts of the rope and pull in whatever direction they want. Say, **If each person on this earth did whatever he or she pleased, there would be chaos. This rope can remind us of everyone doing whatever he or she wants. It might be fun for a while, but it would be dangerous. God calls leaders to maintain order.**

Ask the volunteers holding the ends of the rope to pull the rope straight. The other volunteers will need to yield and form a straight line. Say, **God uses authorities to bring order to the world. He has called Christians to submit to these authorities. The authorities set the course we are to follow: how we act at school, when shopping, while driving, when in public. They bring order. If we wrongfully rebel against them, we also rebel against God.**

Table Talk

(Don't just read—TELL the following true story.)

In 1932, while most German church leaders remained silent, Reverend Hermann Sasse began to preach and write against the teachings and practices of Adolf Hitler and the Nazis. Even after Hitler came to power in 1933 and the state-run churches in Germany agreed to support him, Sasse continued to plead with God's people to distance themselves from the Nazis.

When Wartburg Seminary in Iowa invited Sasse to leave Nazi Germany and teach in America, he said no. He believed that he should stay and try to persuade his countrymen to follow the teachings of Jesus rather than the teachings of Hitler. As dangers increased, many people who disagreed with the Nazis fled to England, Switzerland, or America. Wearied by the constant harassment of the Nazi SS, discouraged because other church leaders would not listen, Sasse also considered leaving.

But just as Sasse decided that he would sneak out of the country and come to the United States, World War II broke out. He could not leave. He stayed at his post as a teacher throughout the war. He watched helplessly as his government imprisoned other pastors and sent his students to die at the front lines.

Discuss one-on-one or in small groups the following questions. (Mentors will guide students through the lesson sheets.)

➡ Student material starts here.

Was it right for Reverend Sasse to speak out against the teachings and practices of the Nazis? Why?

Yes! Since the teachings of the Nazis contradicted God's Word, Reverend Sasse had to speak out.

How do the actions of Reverend Sasse demonstrate his respect for the governing authorities?

Reverend Sasse continued to fulfill his calling to the church and university as a preacher and teacher.

If you disagree with your pastor or government leaders, what should you do?

First, pray for them. Show them from God's Word why you disagree. Protest or take other action only if they refuse to heed God's Word.

Bible Study

In contrast to the worldly authority of the Roman Empire, Jesus teaches His disciples about authority. He shares this teaching just before facing death on the cross for the sins of the world. Read Matthew 20:17–28.

1. According to verses 17–19, how did Jesus show that He was a servant?

He would give His life on the cross.

2. What did the mom in this story think Jesus' kingdom was?

An earthly kingdom.

3. Is there anything wrong with her wanting the best for her sons? Explain.

No. Parents should want the best for their children and should not be afraid to ask God for the best in prayer.

4. In what way are your father and mother wanting the best for you by having you in confirmation study?

They want me to trust God's forgiveness and lead a life pleasing to Him.

5. Can you give an example of someone you know who by serving in a special way demonstrates the love of God and helps motivate others to follow Him?

Answers will vary.

6. Can anyone keep God's Law completely? Why or why not?

Sin corrupts each one of us; therefore, God's Law condemns us all.

7. What does the servant-leadership of Jesus mean for you personally? See 20:28.

He has ransomed my life from sin and death.

Family in Faith Journal

With the help of parents/mentors, students will write a prayer for the pastor and congregational elders, recording it in the Family in Faith Journal.

Fun for Review

Characters: Teacher, Manny, Peggy, Lyn, Willie, Anita, Rick

Setting: Classroom

TEACHER: We're going to work on our assignment as a group. I want you to make a poster with an acrostic.

MANNY: I like doing acrostic puzzles.

PEGGY: Do you mean crossword puzzles?

LYN: An acrostic is when you put a word down the side of the page and each letter stands for something that has to do with that word.

TEACHER: That's right, Lyn.

WILLIE: What is the word we are going to use?

TEACHER: I want you to consider how we are to respect authorities God has placed over us—especially in our church and also in the government.

ANITA: Sometimes it's hard to respect people in government.

RICK: Sometimes it's hard to respect anyone! But I like it when people respect me.

TEACHER: The acrostic word is going to be "R-E-S-P-E-C-T." How and what do we respect in our church and government leaders?

MANNY: Let's start with the letter "R."

LYN: I know—"Rules." God gave the government to rule over us. And the government gives us lots of rules.

PEGGY: And there are rules in church too.

WILLIE: Yeah, like not falling asleep during the sermon. Pastor caught me last week!

ANITA: We need to respect the rules of the government …

RICK: Unless they go against God's rules.

MANNY: Okay, we have "R." What about "E"?

WILLIE: I know! "E" could stand for "Emportant." Church and government are emportant.

PEGGY: I hate to spoil your enthusiasm, but the word "Important" is spelled with an "I," not an "E"!

LYN: How about the word "Encourage"? We respect those in authority by encouraging. They really do have tough jobs.

WILLIE: And we all like to be encouraged in what we are doing.

ANITA: I think for "S" we could use the word "Servant," since pastors and other church workers are servants and people working in government are public servants.

RICK: And I'm ready for "P." Actually, there are three words—"Parents, Pastors, and Politicians." All are people God has placed in authority over us.

ANITA: I like that. Good job!

PEGGY: "E" can stand for "Education." We should respect the education of our leaders, and we should educate ourselves about their work and ministry so we can appreciate them more.

WILLIE: "C" could stand for "Calling." That is spelled with a "C" and not a "K," right?

MANNY: You're learning, Willie, my man!

LYN: They have a calling to serve God and us and we have a calling to respect their work.

WILLIE: This isn't a very fun one, but it can be used when talking about government—"T" could stand for "Taxes."

PEGGY: The Bible does talk about paying our taxes to the authorities.

ANITA: Maybe we could also use the word "Together." God wants us to work together with all whom He has placed in authority over us.

MANNY: That's it. We're finished! That was easy!

WILLIE: Easy? I don't know about you, but I thought that was a very **taxing** assignment!

Finish the Lesson

What makes it difficult to respect leaders in government? Answers will vary. They don't always do what they say they will.

If a pastor leads the congregation, how is he also a servant? The pastor serves both the Lord and the congregation. By proclaiming God's forgiveness to us in Christ, the pastor comforts and encourages us.

Closing Prayer

Focus the attention of the group by reciting "To Bishops, Pastors, and Preachers" and "Of Citizens" responsively (*LSCE*, pp. 33, 35). Then pray the following prayer based on the Table of Duties:

Lord, those who serve You in the church and state are Your gifts to Your people. Help us to show loving respect for those in authority and make their work a joy, not a burden. Forgive us when we wrongfully complain about Your servants; through Christ, our Lord. Amen.

Lesson Suggestions

Hymn: *LW* 371; *TLH* 395; *AGPS* 106

Homework: Have students write a summary paragraph of what they learned or answer the questions in *Exploring Luther's Small Catechism*, pages 8–9.

Memory Work: Assign a verse or verses from the Table of Duties, or use this time to allow students to catch up or work ahead on memory work.

Special Projects: Invite a pastor or elder to address the class on the topic of spiritual care; have students search the media for stories about church–state relations; take a field trip to a police station, court house, military base, or the state capitol to discuss how these agencies serve God.

Fifth Commandment

Focus on the Catechism

Focus the attention of the group by reciting the Fifth Commandment and its meaning responsively (*LSCE,* p. 10). Then pray this or a similar prayer based on the Fifth Commandment:

Lord, You alone give life. You alone hold the right to take life away. Teach us to fear Your power over life and death so that we do no harm to ourselves or those around us. Teach us to love the life You give so that we gladly help and support one another in every physical need; through Jesus Christ. Amen.

Activity

Materials: Old newsmagazines or newspapers, scissors, glue, 2 sheets of poster board

Provide students with copies of old newsmagazines or newspapers. Have them look for examples of people hurting or harming one another. Glue these examples on the first poster board as a collage. Also have the students find examples of people helping and supporting one another. Glue these examples on the second poster board.

Ask, **Was it easier to find examples of people hurting one another or helping one another?** (Hurting.) **Why do you think that is?** Permit students to share their thoughts. Direct them to the problem of sin that corrupts each of us. Say, **In the Fifth Commandment God forbids us to perform violent actions and physical abuse. He calls us to respect the lives of others.**

Table Talk

(Don't just read—TELL the following true story.)

Everyone has heard of Santa Claus or St. Nick. But few have heard the original story that got the Santa Claus legend started. In the fourth-century city of Myra in Asia Minor there lived a pastor named Nicholas, a man who had suffered persecution by the Roman rulers and had shown himself to be faithful to God.

Once, Nicholas overheard that a family with three daughters had lost its fortune. To make ends meet, the family decided to sell their oldest daughter into prostitution. Nicholas sneaked to the family's house and tossed a bag of money through an open window. When the family found the money, they used it for the marriage of the oldest daughter rather than sell her into prostitution. But their financial trouble arose again. This time, the family considered selling the second daughter. Nicholas tossed another bag of money through the family's window and saved the second daughter's life as well. The same thing happened with the third daughter. When people learned what Nicholas had done, they thanked him profusely for his generosity. His gifts had spared the lives of others.

Discuss one-on-one or in small groups the following questions. (Mentors will guide students through the lesson sheets.)

➡ Student material starts here.

According to the catechism's explanation of the Fifth Commandment, how did the decisions of this family contradict God's Word?

Prostitution meant physical harm for their daughters.

How do Nicholas's actions show a clear understanding of the Fifth Commandment?

The Fifth Commandment teaches us to "help and support" our neighbor.

How does the true story of St. Nicholas contrast with modern tales of Santa Claus?

The original story is far more serious and teaches us about God's will rather than our selfish desires. It's about preserving life instead of gratifying our flesh.

Bible Study

The road from Jerusalem to Jericho curves through rocky terrain where robbers can easily hide. Read Luke 10:25–37.

1. According to Old Testament law, priests and Levites were considered "unclean" for several days if they touched a dead man. They could not do their religious work. Would that have made it right for the men to pass by? Explain.

No. The greatest worship is to believe and obey God's Word.

2. Sometimes robbers pretended to be beaten up. When a person stopped to help, the robber would leap up and rob them. Would that have been a good reason to pass by the man in the parable?

No. But we need to be careful in helping others.

3. Considering that the Jews and Samaritans hated each other, what unusual twist does Jesus put into His parable? See Luke 10:33–35.

The Samaritan stops to help an injured Jew. A deeper understanding of the parable shows that Jesus is talking about Himself. Like the Samaritan, Jesus rescued us even when sin made us enemies of God.

4. According to Jesus, who is our neighbor and what would God have us do for him? See Luke 10:36–37.

Answers will vary. Everyone is our neighbor. God calls us to help and support our neighbor in every physical need.

5. Name someone in your school who needs help. Who needs a special friend? Who needs some special words of encouragement?

Answers will vary.

6. How do abortion, euthanasia, and suicide violate the Fifth Commandment?

Each of these involves wrongfully taking a person's life. They do not respect God as the giver of life.

7. Motivated by God's love for those in need, what specifically might I do for someone this week? (Mentors should help to come up with several suggestions.)

Answers will vary.

8. We cannot keep God's Law perfectly. But who has kept the Law perfectly for us and our salvation?

Jesus. He alone can save us.

9. How is Jesus similar to the Good Samaritan?

He rescues us from sin and death. He pays for the support of our life, giving all good things for us.

Family in Faith Journal

Have students recall an injury or illness and their parent's care during the healing process. Offer a prayer of thanks to the heavenly Father for the blessing of healing through Jesus Christ. Parents/mentors should record this memory in the Family in Faith Journal.

Fun for Review

Prop: Newspaper

Characters: Evil Angel, Good Angel, Man, 2 or 3 Thieves, Priest, Levite, Good Samaritan

Setting: The two ANGELS stand next to each other. The MAN is walking on a road, reading a newspaper.

EVIL ANGEL: *(Sneering)* Okay, this is going to be good! Watch what happens.

GOOD ANGEL: *(Wincing and shuddering)* You really shouldn't … I mean, you're really sick!

MAN: *(Mumbling to himself)* Hmmm, it says here, "Watch out for thieves on Jericho Way." Whew! At least I'm not on … wait a minute … yikes!

THIEVES rob him, then exit.

GOOD ANGEL: Wait! I see someone coming in the distance. The way he's dressed … it must be … wait a minute … it is! It's a priest. This man of God will surely help this poor fellow.

The PRIEST quickly passes by.

EVIL ANGEL: There goes your chance, choirboy. And to think only moments ago he was leading people in worship! That's my kind of priest!

GOOD ANGEL: Here comes a blessing! If the priest wouldn't help him, maybe this Levite will. He surely knows God's will. He surely knows to love thy neighbor.

The LEVITE passes by.

EVIL ANGEL: He surely knows how to keep walkin', baby! Yeah, baby! Keep walkin'! *(Laughing)*

GOOD SAMARITAN enters.

GOOD ANGEL: Hmmm. A Samaritan, huh? Samaritans and Jews usually hate each other. I wonder … I just wonder …

EVIL ANGEL: *(Listening to GOOD ANGEL)* You wonder what? You wonder if you're going to lose your job? *(Evil laugh)*

GOOD ANGEL: No. No, I don't. I wonder if the Lord … yep. I wouldn't put it past Him. This is the way He works sometimes, you know.

GOOD SAMARITAN sees the MAN and goes over to help him.

GOOD ANGEL: Thank You, Lord, for saving him. *(Turning to EVIL ANGEL)* And YOU! You little pointy-tail, pitch-fork, devil wannabe! You didn't think it was possible, did you? *(Mocking)* Noooo. Certainly not this Samaritan! Noooo. I guess you forgot about God's words, "Hear, O Israel, the Lord our God, the Lord is one. Love the Lord your God with all your heart and with all your soul and with all your mind and with all your strength." AND, "Love your neighbor as yourself. There is no commandment greater than these."

EVIL ANGEL: I'm mellllllllltiiiiiiing!

GOOD ANGEL: Now get outta here!

EVIL ANGEL: *(Looking into the distance)* Hey! Looks like they're going into an inn. Like he's gonna have enough to pay for all the help that guy needs.

GOOD ANGEL: I put a Visa card in his pocket.

EVIL ANGEL: A what?

GOOD ANGEL: Just give it up, would ya?!

Finish the Lesson

What might prevent you from helping someone in need? My own needs, interests, and concerns may distract me from helping other people.

Is it possible to help someone too much? Explain your answer. Yes. If people become dependent on us for their livelihood, they are not living up to the potential God created them to have.

Closing Prayer

Focus the attention of the group by reciting the Fifth Commandment and its meaning responsively (*LSCE,* p. 10). Then pray this or a similar prayer based on the Fifth Commandment:

Lord, You alone give life. You alone hold the right to take life away. Teach us to fear Your power over life and death so that we do no harm to ourselves or those around us. Teach us to love the life You give so that we gladly help and support one another in every physical need. Forgive us when we fail to care for one another; through Jesus Christ. Amen.

Lesson Suggestions

Hymn: *TLH* 287; *LW* 331:1, 6, 11–12; *AGPS* 82

Homework: *LSCE* questions 52–54. Have students write a summary paragraph of what they learned or answer the questions in *Exploring Luther's Small Catechism*, pages 15–16.

Memory Work: Fifth Commandment; Genesis 9:6 (150); Proverbs 31:8 (155)

Sixth Commandment

Focus on the Catechism

Focus the attention of the group by reciting the Sixth Commandment responsively (*LSCE,* p. 10). Then pray this or a similar prayer based on the commandment:

Lord, You created us male and female. You built the power of life and birth into our bodies. Help us to fear You that we may live a sexually pure and decent life. Help us to love You so that we may love one another and honor the blessings of marriage and sex; through Jesus Christ, our Lord. Amen.

Activity

Materials: Pipe cleaners—one per student, wire cutters

Say, **To help you better understand how to live the sexually pure and decent life intended by God, I am going to give each of you a pipe cleaner.** Tell the students that they are going to make a custom-fit ring for their finger. The students will first twist the ends of the pipe cleaner together. This should make a large ring, too big for their finger. However, have them try it on. It obviously will need adjusting. Say, **In the Sixth Commandment God requires us to avoid sexual temptations and to be clean in what we think and say. Sexual intercourse doesn't fit outside of marriage any better than this large ring fits on a finger.**

Have the students twist the large ring in the center, making it half its original size. Again the ring should be too large for a student's finger. However, have students try it on again. Tell them that until they marry as God intends, they are to keep themselves sexually pure. Say, **God intends marriage to be a lifelong union between one man and one woman. Don't rush, but take that commitment seriously.**

The ring should again be placed on the finger and twisted to fit. After a good fit has been achieved, cut off the excess wire. You will need to use strong scissors or wire cutters. Say, **God intends sexual intercourse exclusively for marriage as a demonstration of the oneness and commitment of a man and a woman. Let the ring you wear after marriage remind you of the discussion in this activity and of the Sixth Commandment.**

Table Talk

(Don't just read—TELL the following true story.)

Dr. Bessie Rehwinkel, one of the first women doctors on the American frontier, faced a painful decision. A young woman came to her with a problem: she was pregnant and she had no husband. The young woman had been engaged to a farmer from her neighborhood, and they had planned to get married within the year. As they waited for the wedding, they decided that it would be alright to have sex since they would surely get married anyway. But then the young man suddenly got sick. He died, leaving his fiancé pregnant.

The young woman tearfully pleaded with Dr. Bessie to perform an abortion for her. The doctor felt torn between her sorrow for the woman's plight and her own sense of duty as a doctor. Could this young woman have guessed that she would get pregnant, that she would suddenly lose her fiancé, that she would face life on the frontier as a single mother? But then Dr. Bessie explained that abortion can be a dangerous operation, destroying a woman's ability to have more children. What's more, the child within her had done nothing to deserve death. Though this young woman now faced personal hardship, should her child die because of her mistake?

Discuss one-on-one or in small groups the following questions. (Mentors will guide students through the lesson sheets.)

➡ <u>Student material starts here.</u>

How did sex before marriage add to this young woman's sorrow and hardship?

She got pregnant unexpectedly.

Is sex before marriage always wrong? Explain your answer.

Yes. Students should recognize that even when sex does not result in unexpected pregnancy or disease, it still creates a strong physical bond between two people. God designed this bond for the commitment of marriage alone.

In view of this story, why did God give us the Sixth Commandment?

To protect us from trouble and emotional damage. Also to protect children.

Bible Study

King David rules Israel. Instead of leading his men, David stays at the palace and falls into temptation. Read 2 Samuel 11:1–15, 26–27.

1. What sexual sin did David commit?

Adultery.

2. In what way is this story like a snowball rolling down a large hill of fresh, sticky snow? Read James 1:15. How was David's sin much like the description given by James?

David's sin starts out with lust. Then it turns into adultery. Then he resorts to murder!

3. Can you describe a time when some small, sinful desire took over your life and became bigger and bigger with time?

Answers will vary.

4. How might the Sixth Commandment apply to homosexuality and pornography?

Homosexual sex is sinful. It goes against God's design for life. Pornography degrades God's gift of sex and encourages lust and abuse.

5. List everything you learned in this lesson about God's gift of sexuality. Circle the one fact you did not know before you came to class. Underline the one thing on the list you think you might someday have the most difficulty obeying. Explain why.

Answers will vary.

6. Read David's confession of his sin with Bathsheba as recorded in Psalm 51:10–12. Where do we also find forgiveness for the sexual sins we commit?

Students may recognize this passage from the worship service. God's Word and Sacrament grant us the forgiveness Jesus Christ won for us.

7. Does having God's forgiveness mean that the consequences of our sin immediately go away? Read 2 Samuel 12:13–14.

No. Our sins have consequences for other people. For example, the child born of David's adultery died as a result of David's sin.

8. No matter how hard we try, we fail to keep our hearts and thoughts pure from lust. Who alone can keep this commandment purely and take away our sin?

Jesus. The Law can never save us. Our only hope of forgiveness and salvation is in Christ.

Family in Faith Journal

Parents/mentors should describe how they first met their spouses and fell in love. What place does God's love have in that relationship? Have students summarize the story in the Family in Faith Journal.

Fun for Review

Characters: Big Brother, Little Brother, Bird, Bee

Setting: Family Room

BIG BROTHER: *(Motioning to chair)* Little brother, have a seat. It's time we had a little talk.

LITTLE BROTHER: *(Sitting down)* Oh, no. I don't like the sound of this.

BIG BROTHER: *(Pacing back and forth)* Well, it's time we had this talk.

LITTLE BROTHER: You said that already, big brother.

BIG BROTHER: I did? Oh, yeah. I'm just a little nervous. Well. The talk. Ummm. Little brother …

LITTLE BROTHER: Yes?

BIG BROTHER: I want to talk to you about the, ummm …

LITTLE BROTHER: Yes?

BIG BROTHER: Well, you're getting older now, and you need to know about the birds and the bees.

LITTLE BROTHER: *(Softly mumbling)* Oh, I should have known—the sex talk.

BIG BROTHER: What's that, little brother?

LITTLE BROTHER: Umm, I said I should have taken Rex for a walk.

BIG BROTHER: I just took him out. Besides, I want to have this talk about the birds and the bees.

LITTLE BROTHER: Okay, okay … the birds and the bees.

BIG BROTHER: It goes like this … *(BIG BROTHER paces and pretends to be talking to LITTLE BROTHER as the BIRD and BEE do their part.)*

BIRD: *(Flies into room)* Tweet. Tweet. Tweet.

BEE: *(Flies into room)* Buzzz. Buzzzz. Buzzzz.

BIRD: Cheep. Cheep.

BEE: Hmmmmmm. Hmmmmmm.

BIRD: Cheep. Cheep. Tweet. Tweet.

BEE: Buzzzz. Buzzz. Buzzz. Sting!

BIG BROTHER: And that's what I wanted to tell you.

LITTLE BROTHER: *(Sarcastic)* That's, well, what should I say? That's very helpful, big brother.

BIG BROTHER: I'm glad, little brother.

LITTLE BROTHER: I was being sarcastic. That didn't help me at all.

BIG BROTHER: Oh?

LITTLE BROTHER: Mom and Dad already talked with me about sex. You don't have to disguise the subject by using birds and bees. I know that it's a wonderful gift from God. It's an emotional and physical gift to be shared joyfully only within marriage. Within relationships, a man and a woman need to respect each other and keep Christ their focus as they grow together in His love.

BIG BROTHER: What?! They told you already?

LITTLE BROTHER: I also learned about sex in confirmation, in a short story told by a German shepherd.

BIG BROTHER: A German shepherd? And you thought the birds and bees were out of line?

LITTLE BROTHER: Here's what the German shepherd says: "We should fear and love God so that we lead a sexually pure and decent life in what we say and do, and husband and wife love and honor each other."

BIG BROTHER: Wait a minute. That's what Martin Luther wrote about the Sixth Commandment.

LITTLE BROTHER: Right! Luther was a German shepherd—a German pastor. "Pastor" means shepherd.

BIG BROTHER: And the "German shepherd" told us what the Bible says about sex and relationships. I still like the birds and the bees.

BIRD: *(Flies into room)* Tweet. Tweet. Tweet.

BEE: *(Flies into room)* Buzzz. Buzzzz. Buzzzz.

BIRD: Cheep. Cheep.

BEE: Hmmmmmm. Hmmmmmm.

Finish the Lesson

How have ideas about sex changed in recent years? People talk a lot more about sex. You see it more on TV and the Internet. However, people seem to be much more cautious about *having* sex. AIDS has made people realize the danger of sex outside of marriage.

In what way is sex a good gift from God? Sex binds two people together and brings forth life.

Explain the role of Word and Sacrament in helping us lead sexually pure lives. Through the Word and Sacraments, God forgives my lust and other sexual sins. Note well! If someone gets pregnant by breaking the Sixth Commandment, she and her boyfriend should not turn to abortion as a way of covering up their sin. Protect the life of the child! Only God's forgiveness can take away sin and enable us to lead lives that please Him.

Closing Prayer

Focus the attention of the group by reciting the Sixth Commandment responsively (*LSCE*, p. 10). Then pray this or a similar prayer based on the commandment:

Lord, You created us male and female. You built the power of life and birth into our bodies. Help us to fear You that we may live a sexually pure and decent life. Help us to love You so that we may love one another and honor the blessings of marriage and sex. Forgive us when we sin against you in thought, word, or deed; through Jesus Christ, our Lord. Amen.

Lesson Suggestions

Hymn: *LW* 331:1, 7, 11–12; *TLH* 287; *AGPS* 240

Homework: *LSCE* questions 55–58. Have students write a summary paragraph of what they learned or answer the questions in *Exploring Luther's Small Catechism,* pages 16–17.

Memory Work: Sixth Commandment; Hebrews 13:4 (174); 1 Corinthians 7:4 (191)

Table of Duties, Home and Work

Focus on the Catechism

Have the boys pray responsively "To Husbands," the girls pray "To Wives," the parents/mentors pray "To Parents," and all the students pray "To Children" (*LSCE*, p. 36). Conclude with the following prayer based on the Table of Duties:

O Father, Son, and Holy Spirit, our Creator, Redeemer, and Sanctifier, You work each day on our behalf. Grant us God-pleasing work and a holy desire to serve others with our bodies and our minds. Help us to recognize our calling in life; through Jesus Christ, our Lord. Amen.

Activity

Materials: Various types and sizes of shoes—some too small for class members and some too large

Say, **God calls each of us to different roles throughout our lives. You have lived as a child and student. Someday you may live as a worker or parent. There may also be other roles you are given. Can you think of any?** List student suggestions on the board. Say, **These shoes can remind us of the different roles we will fill throughout our life.** Have volunteers model the different types of shoes. Some students will be able to walk easily while others should struggle because their shoes are too large or too small.

Say, **We each have different roles to fill throughout life. However, these roles will change. Sometimes we outgrow a role. You will not be students and children forever. However, you are not adults yet either. Trying to fit into roles at the wrong time will make life difficult. Trying to be something you are not is not God's plan. God knows exactly when you are ready for the different roles you will fill during your lifetime.**

The Table of Duties offers verses that will help you understand how to fit into the different roles to which God may call you. If you disregard God's Word concerning your roles in life, you will stumble just as if you were trying to wear shoes that do not fit. Following God's Word concerning different roles will ensure a good fit, just like a good-fitting pair of shoes. We can trust God to help us find and fulfill roles that honor Him. Jesus, our Savior, will remain with us and by His Spirit enable us to serve Him in whatever roles we fill.

Table Talk

(Don't just read—TELL the following true story.)

In 1546 Katherina mourned by the grave of her husband, Martin Luther, the famous reformer of the church. But Martin's death was only the beginning of Katherina's heartache. The local chancellor challenged her husband's will, threatening to take away much of her property. She had run out of money and the elector had approved a plan to take her sons away from her. Despite years of hard work through boarding students for Wittenberg University and caring for the sick, Katherina was in danger of losing her home of 21 years.

Just when it appeared that Katherina's family would fall apart, friends and colleagues that she and her husband had helped and cared for over the years began to send money. They intervened with the local rulers so that Luther's will was upheld and Katherina could keep all her children. In that moment, God's mercy rescued her. Though the troubles that Katherina faced at the time of her husband's death would not be the last that she faced, she saw with her own eyes how the heavenly Father holds families together.

Discuss one-on-one or in small groups the following questions. (Mentors will guide students through the lesson sheets.)

➡ Student material starts here.

What difference did Katherina's service to others make in her life?

As Katherina followed God's Word and served others, God blessed her through the help the people readily gave her.

Who among your family and friends could you count on for help?

Answers will vary.

Does God need our good works? Explain.

No. The almighty God has no need of our good works. However, God desires that we do good works to help our neighbors.

In your own words, what does the Table of Duties teach about the purpose and duty of the following people: (a) husbands, (b) wives, (c) parents, (d) children, (e) workers of all kinds, (f) employers and supervisors?

Discuss the different roles God gives to each. Remind students that slavery was common in the past. But Christianity has encouraged freedom and mutual respect between all people.

Bible Study

Ruth and Naomi's husbands have died. They are poor and face severe hardship, even starvation. Read Ruth 2:2–23; 4:9–10.

1. What did Boaz quickly recognize in Ruth? See 2:11–12.

He recognized her love and devotion for her family.

2. Contrast Ruth's care for her mother-in-law with what happens in today's society with many destitute people. What programs are in place to help them? What about in your church?

Answers will vary.

3. Why is Ruth 1:16–17 such a great summary of the whole story of the Book of Ruth?

She was devoted to go wherever Naomi went in order to help her.

4. Who in your family or other relationships is loyal to you like Ruth was to her mother-in-law? How have you been blessed through their loyalty and love for you?

Answers will vary.

5. What do husband and wife promise to do in their marriage vows? What does this teach about divorce?

They commit to each other for life. Divorce goes against God's will for our lives. Though divorce may be necessary in some cases, God wants families to stay together (see LSCE, question 56).

6. Sin tears at every family. Who alone can rescue your family from division?

Through the blessings of forgiveness, Jesus heals and preserves us. He alone can save us.

7. Since God is our heavenly Father, what does that mean for our families?

We have an ever-present help in time of need. The greatest blessing He provides is forgiveness through His Son.

Family in Faith Journal

Studies tell us that many people feel they have no purpose in life. They don't know why they're here on earth. They don't know if life has any meaning. With parents/mentors, students should write out their purpose and reason for living as a child of God in Christ.

Fun for Review

Characters: Cissy (4 years old), Bobby (3 years old)

Setting: Anywhere

(The sketch will be enhanced if characters talk and act like little children.)

CISSY: Bobby, what are you going to be when you grow up?

BOBBY: I'm not gonna grow up. I'm always gonna be three.

CISSY: You have to grow up.

BOBBY: Do not!

CISSY: Do too! *If* you grow up, what do you want to be?

BOBBY: I'm gonna drive the big truck that picks up our garbage.

CISSY: That's a stinky job.

BOBBY: You're stinky!

CISSY: Am not!

BOBBY: Are too! There's nothing wrong with drivin' the big truck. I bet when you grow up, you'll be happy to see me take away your trash. Otherwise your whole yard and house will be stinky. Without me, you'll be a stinky family with stinky garbage.

CISSY: Will not!

BOBBY: Will too! Stinky! Stinky! Stinky!

CISSY: Okay, I guess that's a 'portant job. I don't want to stink up my house with trash.

BOBBY: What kind of job are you going to have?

CISSY: I'm going to be a mommy.

BOBBY: A mommy? That's not a real job.

CISSY: Is too! My mom works hard. She takes care of me. She loves me and my daddy. Mommy work isn't easy. My mom cooks, drives me places, plays games with me, and even cleans the bathroom.

BOBBY: She likes doing that?

CISSY: She likes being a mommy, and that's what I want to be. Just like my mommy or … maybe a ballerina.

BOBBY: Are you going to get married to a boy?

CISSY: Sounds yucky, but I guess I will have to. I'm not going to like being around boys until I'm like, really old. You know … 30 or 40.

BOBBY: Boys aren't yucky. Girls are.

CISSY: Are not!

BOBBY: Are too!

(Pause.)

BOBBY: I think I'm going to pick up some trash around the house. That will be good practice for when I clean with the big truck someday.

CISSY: And I think I'll practice being a mommy.

BOBBY: Okay.

CISSY: Hey, why do we have to be anything at all? Do I have to work?

BOBBY: Sure! Everyone has to work, 'cause God made it that way. 'Member what He said to Adam and Eve? They had to take care of the garden.

CISSY: I 'member … and they had to get married and have babies too.

BOBBY: That's *really* yucky!

Finish the Lesson

Why is work or vocation important for you as a Christian? Our heavenly Father created us for work. He gives each of us special talents to serve Him and others.

How will God's Word help you honor Him in whatever vocation you choose? God's Word guides not only our "spirituality," but every aspect of our lives. His Word will keep you focused on what is truly important.

Closing Prayer

Have the boys pray responsively "To Husbands," the girls pray "To Wives," the parents/mentors pray "To Parents," and all the students pray "To Children" (*LSCE*, p. 36). Conclude with the following prayer based on the Table of Duties:

Father Creator, Son Redeemer, Spirit Sanctifier, You work each day on our behalf. Grant us God-pleasing work and a holy desire to serve others with our bodies and our minds. Help us to recognize our calling in life and forgive us when we fail; through Jesus Christ, our Lord. Amen.

Lesson Suggestions

Hymn: *LW* 467:l; *TLH* 625; *AGPS* 191

Homework: Have students write a summary paragraph of what they learned.

Memory Work: Ephesians 6:1–3 (*LSCE*, p. 36)

Special Projects: Bring in a panel of newly engaged as well as mature couples to talk about faith and marriage; invite a high school guidance counselor to discuss vocation; make a special effort to recruit students for volunteer service at church (usher, acolyte, teaching) or full-time church work.

8 Seventh Commandment

Focus on the Catechism

Focus the attention of the group by reciting the Seventh Commandment responsively (*LSCE,* p. 11). Then pray this or a similar prayer based on the commandment:

Lord, You entrust each of us with our possessions. Teach us to fear Your wrath so that we do not rob our neighbors. Teach us to love You for Your generosity and to generously improve and protect our neighbors' possessions and income; through Christ. Amen.

Activity

Materials: Advertisement clippings, tape, dartboard, darts

Before class collect advertisements for popular items like CD players, clothing, bikes, Rollerblades—anything you know the students in your class would consider valuable. It would be best if you have duplicate pictures of some of the items. You will also need a dartboard and a few darts.

Hold up the pictures and ask if the students have friends who have some of these items. Attach a few of the items to the dartboard. Say, **Each of us has opportunities from time to time to borrow or share a friend's possessions. It is important that we respect and take care of these items.** Ask for a volunteer to come and throw the darts at the board. Say, **By throwing these darts, you realize you will make holes in these pictures.** The darts will hit the pictures and poke holes in them. Say, **When we are careless with a friend's possessions, it's similar to how we treated these pictures. It may seem funny or a small matter to damage someone's belongings, but God calls us to protect those things that belong to others.** Take the remaining pictures and tape them to the back of the dartboard. Again ask for a volunteer. Allow the volunteer to throw darts at the front of the dartboard.

After a few darts are thrown, remove the pictures from the back of the board. Say, **The dartboard protected these pictures. It took the hit from the dart, and the board did not let the dart touch the picture. God calls us to be in the position of the dartboard when we are using something that belongs to someone else. We are to defend and protect those things we are using that belong to someone else. At times it may be uncomfortable or even difficult to show respect for borrowed items, but the Seventh Commandment forbids us to intentionally harm those things that belong to our neighbor. How can you serve as a dartboard and protect items you have borrowed?** Make a list of suggestions on the board.

Table Talk

(Don't just read—TELL the following true story.)

According to the Better Business Bureau, someone shoplifts at a store every five seconds. Businesses lose an estimated $16 billion each year to shoplifters. Employees commit 70 percent of the shoplifting. One third of all businesses fail because of the high cost of retail theft.

Who cares? You care! Here's why: For every dollar you spend in a store, 5 to 10 cents goes to pay for things other people steal. That means you pay hundreds of dollars each year because other people steal from the stores where you shop. Half of all people who shoplift are teenagers—your peers. The next time you're in a store and can't buy something because it costs too much, remember why it costs so much: thieves.

Discuss one-on-one or in small groups the following questions. (Mentors will guide students through the lesson sheets.)

➡ Student material starts here.

How do shoplifters affect your life?

They make everything more expensive.

If a friend asked you to help him/her shoplift, what might you say?

Answers will vary. The student may explain why stealing is wrong and why it hurts others.

Is it okay to steal if you really need something? Explain.

No. Instead of stealing, one should ask for help.

How does stealing show a lack of fear and trust for God?

God promises to take care of our needs. If we steal, we show that we don't fear His wrath or trust His promise.

Bible Study

As a tax collector, Zacchaeus demands more taxes from the people in his region so that he can make himself rich. Jesus visits Zacchaeus's community and preaches about God's kingdom. Read Luke 19:1–10.

1. How did Zacchaeus's actions break the Seventh Commandment?

He collected more money than he was supposed to.

2. If Zacchaeus used the money he collected for a worthy cause, would that make everything okay? Explain.

No. He would still be stealing.

3. Reread verse 8. How did Zacchaeus's actions back up his newfound faith?

He wanted to demonstrate that his faith was genuine and help those whom he had hurt by repaying them as the Old Testament prescribed.

4. Share a time with one another when you felt repentant for something you had done and tried to make up for the wrongdoing in a way similar to Zacchaeus.

Answers will vary.

5. Though some were angry with Jesus for going to Zacchaeus's house, what did Jesus teach them about His mission?

He came to seek and to save the lost.

6. Why are you personally glad Jesus came to seek and to save sinners?

Because I'm a sinner. I don't keep God's commandments as I should; therefore, I need His salvation too.

Family in Faith Journal

Have students list things they share at home. Make a second list of things they don't share and discuss why they don't. Talk about how Jesus would have us use our possessions. Record these thoughts in the Family in Faith Journal.

Fun for Review

Characters: 3 Complainers, Zacchaeus, Jesus

Setting: ZACCHAEUS walks by on his way to his tax booth. He takes a seat and begins counting coins. COMPLAINERS stand nearby.

COMPLAINER 1: (*Sarcastically*) Well, there goes his "excellency," Zacchaeus the Zucchini.

COMPLAINER 2: How much do you owe him this time?

COMPLAINER 1: About 50 denarii! That's not nearly as much as it used to be, but it's still too much.

COMPLAINER 3: Whatever happened to old Zucchini, anyway? Why the sudden change in tax policy? Is he trying to trick us somehow?

COMPLAINER 1: Didn't you hear? He's got religion. Remember when Jesus passed through town, preaching about the kingdom of God? He stayed at Zucchini's house. He's been acting suspiciously ever since.

COMPLAINER 2: Yeah. He gave back some of my tax money. And he gave four times as much to Widow Sarah. Ever since he met Jesus, he's been smiling and friendly. He's gone through a big change.

COMPLAINER 1: But he's still a "wee little man" in my eyes! People don't change like that. Zucchini's up to something. He'll squash every tax dollar out of us that he can.

ALL COMPLAINERS: (*Turn toward ZACCHAEUS and shake fists.*) Squasher! (*Exit singing "Zucchini was a wee little man."*)

ZACCHAEUS: (*Looking sad*) When I charged too much for taxes, they didn't trust me. Now that I've repaid people, they're still suspicious. Why do I even bother?

JESUS: (*Enters behind ZACCHAEUS*) You bother because your stealing bothered Me.

ZACCHAEUS: (*Surprised*) Jesus?

JESUS: And your stealing didn't just bother Me. It bothered others as well. Think about Widow Sarah. Because of high taxes, she had nothing to feed her children.

ZACCHAEUS: Yeah, I remember, nothing but squash!

JESUS: And your other neighbors, aren't they better off now?

ZACCHAEUS: (*Growing cheerful*) Yes, now they have extra money to improve and protect their possessions and income. Everyone's better off. (*Growing sad*) Everyone but me.

JESUS: God's commandments aren't just about you, Zach. They're about everyone. Before we met, you only thought of yourself and your possessions. Now that you fear and love God, you care about your neighbors as well. Not everyone understands yet. But give them some time to see the difference God can make.

ALL COMPLAINERS: (*Enter singing*) Zucchini was a wee little man and a wee little man was he!

COMPLAINER 1: (*Interrupting*) Hey! Isn't that Jesus talking with Zucchini again?

COMPLAINER 3: I wonder what they're up to. Probably some new tax scheme. I hear that Jesus wants to start a kingdom of His own. He probably needs the money.

ALL COMPLAINERS: (*Turn toward ZACCHAEUS and JESUS, shaking fists.*) Squashers! (*Exit.*)

JESUS: Well, Zach, since I came to seek and to save the lost, it looks like I have some more work to do. (*Calling after COMPLAINERS*) Wait up! Let Me tell you about a kingdom without taxes.

Finish the Lesson

If you had stolen something from one of your neighbors and you wanted to return it, do you think that would be difficult? Why? Yes. They would probably be angry at first.

How might it change things between you and your neighbor? The neighbor would probably be angry. However, afterward he or she might have greater respect for you because you were honest.

Closing Prayer

Focus the attention of the group by reciting the Seventh Commandment responsively (*LSCE,* p. 11). Then pray this or a similar prayer based on the commandment:

Lord, You entrust each of us with our possessions. Teach us to fear Your wrath so that we do not rob our neighbors. Teach us to love You for Your generosity and to generously improve and protect our neighbors' possessions and income. Please forgive us when we sin against others in thought, word, and deed; through Christ. Amen.

Lesson Suggestions

Hymns: *LW* 331:1, 8, 11–12; *TLH* 287; *AGPS* 191

Homework: *LSCE* questions 59–60. Have students write a summary paragraph of what they learned or answer the questions in *Exploring Luther's Small Catechism,* page 18.

Memory Work: Seventh Commandment; Ephesians 4:28 (196); Hebrews 13:16 (201)

9

Eighth Commandment

Focus on the Catechism

Focus the attention of the group by reciting the Eighth Commandment responsively (*LSCE,* p. 11). Then pray this or a similar prayer based on the commandment:

Lord, Your Word tells the truth and condemns all falsehood. May we fear Your wrath so that we do not lie. Strengthen us in Your love so that we encourage our neighbors through Christ, our Lord. Amen.

Activity

Materials: Balloons, pins, tape

Have each student blow up a balloon and tie it off. Ask students to think of a student at school who gets picked on. Ask, **What makes a student unpopular or what causes a student to be picked on?** Let students share their answers. Pass out a pin to each student. Explain that each time a person is "picked on" or teased it is like a pin going into them. Have the students stick the pin into their balloons. Discuss the damage caused by teasing and mocking.

Say, **The Eighth Commandment teaches that we are to "help and support our neighbor." That means God wants us to be merciful, kind, and forgiving.** Have students inflate another balloon and tie it off. Brainstorm ways to help and support students who are picked on. Now give each student four pieces of tape. Say, **The Eighth Commandment makes it clear that we are to help and support others, including the people who are "picked on" and teased.** Have the students place the four pieces of tape in a criss-cross pattern on the balloon. Now slowly poke the pin though the four pieces of tape and into the balloon. The balloon will not pop, but will stay inflated, at least for a while. Say, **The Eighth Commandment reminds us that helping and supporting our neighbors gives them special strength. We all need strength. Who in your school or neighborhood or even in this church needs the special strength your friendship can provide?**

Table Talk

(Don't just read—TELL the following true story.)

Nick Nicholson always left his audiences in tears. At funerals, business luncheons, and school assemblies, he gripped people's hearts with his speeches about serving as a Green Beret in Vietnam. His chest full of medals stirred his listeners' pride.

But only a month after receiving the Distinguished Service Cross, the second highest U.S. military honor, investigators discovered that Nicholson was lying! While others faced death in Vietnam, Nicholson had worked as a security guard in Florida. Formerly Nicholson had moved people to tears of pride, but now he moved them to tears of bitter anger and shame.

According to investigators, hundreds of men have claimed that they served in Vietnam when in fact they have never served in the military. Some criminals have even claimed that they committed their crimes because of trauma they experienced in Vietnam. As a result, when real veterans sought to build a war memorial in Texas, they could not raise enough money for the project because not enough people believed that they were genuine veterans.

Discuss one-on-one or in small groups the following questions. (Mentors will guide students through the lesson sheets.)

➡ Student material starts here.

How did Nick Nickolson's dishonesty affect the lives of other people?

He actually destroyed the reputations of many veterans.

Do you think people will trust Nick Nicholson again? Why?

Not likely. Honesty is the foundation of trust.

Is it possible to tell lies and never get caught?

God sees and hears all we do and say. Even when we think that we get away with a lie, we cannot escape God's judgment.

Bible Study

Just before His arrest, Jesus stays at the home of Simon, a Pharisee. Mary enters the room unexpectedly and anoints Him. Read Mark 14:3–11.

1. Why did Jesus welcome Mary's action? See 14:7–9.

It was a sincere expression of love.

2. How do the thoughts of some of the people go against the Eighth Commandment?

They did not try to "explain everything in the kindest way" but slandered her.

3. Share with one another insulting words that have been spoken to you that have stayed with you over the years (e.g., shrimp, fatso, homo). How did these words make you feel? What kind of words have you spoken to others in the last week that you wish you could take back?

Answers will vary.

4. What words might cheer up someone who is having a bad day?

Answers will vary.

5. Give an example of how you might defend someone's reputation this week. How might you speak up for someone this week?

Answers will vary.

6. Reread verse 8. In what way did Jesus' life, death, burial, and resurrection rescue us from those words we've spoken that have been unkind and have hurt other people?

The truth of the Gospel erases our sinful thoughts and words.

7. As a sinner, how does the way Jesus spoke to Mary encourage you?

Jesus gladly forgave Mary despite her many sins. Therefore, I know that I can always count on His forgiveness and mercy.

Family in Faith Journal

Come up with five specific compliments for your student. Include a compliment for the student's service or devotion at church. The student should record the compliments in the Family in Faith Journal.

Fun for Review

Characters: Editor, Reporter 1, Reporter 2, Reporter 3

Setting: Staff meeting of The National Informant

EDITOR: So, staff, what story ideas do we have for the special school issue of *The National Informant*?

REPORTER 1: I spent the week at the junior high school on the west side of town.

EDITOR: What do you have?

REPORTER 1: I heard some girls talking about another chick in their class who they say stole some earrings. It sounds like she's a straight "A" student and they want her to get in trouble. She's smart but ugly. The way they talked, no one liked her.

EDITOR: Did you talk to anyone else, or are you just taking their word for it?

REPORTER 1: I don't know anything for sure, but who cares?

REPORTER 2: Well, I spent time at a different junior high school. I heard some students at a lunch table laughing about a teacher they can't stand. I think they said something about him going to a shrink three times a week. He's probably psycho!

EDITOR: Are you sure they said "shrink"? Maybe he's a skater and goes to the "rink" three times a week. You know you don't hear very well.

REPORTER 2: Shrink … rink. Who cares?

EDITOR: Okay, what else do we have?

REPORTER 3: I spent the last couple of days at this Christian school. Talk about bizarre stories.

EDITOR: Tell us!

REPORTER 3: The teachers were telling the kids about some baby born of a virgin! Great headline material, huh? But that's not all. I guess the parents are really poor and don't have insurance, so they keep the baby in a barn. Get this—the baby sleeps in a feeding trough for the animals!

REPORTER 2: Good scoop, Scooter!

EDITOR: I'm not so sure about this. What else did you hear?

REPORTER 3: It seems this baby grows up. People make fun of Him, make up lies about Him, betray and slander Him, and try to hurt His reputation. But it doesn't end there—they kill Him. And while He's dying, He forgives the people who kill Him!

EDITOR: This is too bizarre!

REPORTER 3: The way I overheard it, this guy dies out of love for others, hoping that as He loved them, they will love one another. So that instead of lying and ruining people's reputations, they will explain everything in the kindest way and not slander and …

EDITOR: Okay, we've heard enough of that garbage. I know we've done some wild stories, but this is too wild.

REPORTER 2: Like that one where the alien with only a head gives birth to a laptop computer.

REPORTER 1: Hey, that was one of my best stories!

EDITOR: Let's go with the story about the girl who stole the earrings for the cover story. But you don't have any reliable sources?

REPORTER 1: Since when did we care about reliable sources? When did we begin caring about hurting someone's feelings or reputation?

EDITOR: Good point. Let's go with it. And then let's follow up with the story about the teacher. Add some stuff that makes them both look really bad, okay?

REPORTERS 1 and 2: You can count on us, boss. You can count on us.

Finish the Lesson

How does gossip affect your friendships? Answers will vary.

If someone has started rumors about you, what would Jesus have you do? The Lord wants us to speak directly with those who offend us. Let the person know how his or her words have caused you harm. Ask for the Lord's help to forgive.

Closing Prayer

Focus the attention of the group by reciting the Eighth Commandment responsively (*LSCE*, p. 11). Then pray this or a similar prayer based on the commandment:

Lord, Your Word tells the truth and condemns all falsehood. May we fear Your wrath so that we do not lie. Forgive us when we fail to tell the truth. Strengthen us in Your love so that we encourage our neighbors through Christ, our Lord. Amen.

Lesson Suggestions

Hymn: *LW* 331:1, 9, 11–12; *TLH* 287; *AGPS* 187

Homework: *LSCE* questions 61–62. Have students write a summary paragraph of what they learned or answer the questions in *Exploring Luther's Small Catechism*, page 19.

Memory Work: Eighth Commandment; Proverbs 11:13 (205); Matthew 18:15 (206)

10 Ninth and Tenth Commandments

Focus on the Catechism

Focus the attention of the group by reciting the Ninth and Tenth Commandments responsively (*LSCE,* p. 11). Then pray this or a similar prayer based on the commandments:

Triune God—Father, Son, and Holy Spirit—You created our hearts and minds. Teach us to fear Your wrath so we don't scheme against our neighbors. Teach us to love You so that we use our hearts and minds to encourage one another. Amen.

Activity

Materials: 2 buckets, variety of weighty items, set of weights labeled "Thanks"

Have a volunteer hold the two buckets. A second volunteer should begin filling one of the buckets as you speak. Say, **Because of sin in our hearts, we always want more. We load up our lives with possessions. We envy those who have more. We work and slave to collect the most.** As the bucket fills, it will become more difficult for the volunteer to hold it. As the volunteer leans to one side, ask the class, **What's wrong? Why is _____ leaning?** The volunteer has become off balance because too much weight is on one side. Have the second volunteer begin adding "thanks" weights to the other bucket.

Say, **God wants us to balance our desires with genuine thanksgiving.** Fill the bucket until the person is back in balance. Ask the person holding the buckets, **How are you doing? Are the buckets getting heavy?** (Yes.) **Would you like to give some of that away?** As you unload the buckets and pass out the contents to the other students, say, **God created us for a balanced life. His Ninth and Tenth Commandments teach us about a life of balance and contentment, thanking God for what we have instead of coveting the possessions of others.**

Table Talk

(Don't just read—TELL the following true story.)

In early June, Boniface rested beside the quiet waters of the River Borne in Holland. He and his companions awaited a group of students who had agreed to meet them by the river for confirmation classes.

Thirty-eight years earlier, Boniface had left England to start mission work among the Frisians of Holland. But the Frisians were not ready to listen to Boniface's message. So he traveled throughout northwestern Europe, proclaiming the Gospel and teaching the catechism among the various Germanic tribes. So many people came to faith through his work that people called Boniface "the apostle of Germany."

When he was about 80 years old, Boniface returned to Frisia to gather students, hoping once again to share the love of Christ among the Frisians. But as Boniface rested by the river that day, he was not greeted by his students, but by thieves. Some of the local tribesmen had seen Boniface and his companions set up their tents. They assumed these travelers must be wealthy. Therefore, they attacked and killed an 80-year-old man, only to search his tent and find a few books.

Discuss one-on-one or in small groups the following questions. (Mentors will guide students through the lesson sheets.)

➡ Student material starts here.

How were the desires of Boniface and the Frisian tribesmen different?

Boniface desired to share the Gospel with the tribesmen. But the tribesmen coveted Boniface's possessions.

How did the thoughts of Boniface and the tribesmen change their actions?

Boniface traveled and faced danger in order to share the message of God's love and forgiveness. The tribesmen killed and stole.

If you scheme to get what belongs to someone else but never carry out your plan, have you broken the Ninth or Tenth Commandments? Explain.

Yes. Because God understands that sin begins in our hearts long before we act, He commands us to have pure thoughts and desires.

Bible Study

Ahab is king of Samaria and Naboth is one of his subjects. Read 1 Kings 21.

1. Was it wrong for Ahab to want to buy Naboth's vineyard? When did Ahab begin to sin?

No. Ahab sinned when he became angry and coveted Naboth's vineyard.

2. In what way does verse 5 reflect how some people act when they don't get what they want?

We often sulk when someone turns us down. Such an attitude does not please God, who wants us to rejoice in what we have.

3. Can you name a time when you sulked over something you didn't get?

Answers will vary.

4. What happened when you sulked? Did you get what you wanted?

Answers will vary. Sulking should not be rewarded.

5. Define in your own words the meaning of "coveting." Give some personal examples of when you've coveted.

Coveting means to desire something wrongfully, to scheme after something that doesn't belong to you.

6. Reread 21:28–29. Why might God bring punishment for Ahab's sin on the next generation?

Although Ahab had repented of this sin, his actions were viewed and copied by his children (1 Kings 22:51–53). Lord, break the cycle of sin in our families!

7. Read or recall the opening words of Psalm 23. Where can you find true contentment?

True contentment comes from the Lord. We trust His promise to take care of all our needs, especially the need for forgiveness. He is the only Savior.

8. How might knowing Christ grant you contentment?

Through Christ I have God's forgiveness. That's more important and more satisfying than all material possessions. His love lasts eternally.

Family in Faith Journal

Have students record a time when they really wanted something and didn't get it (e.g., a Christmas present). How might they see things differently now in light of the commandments and the life of Jesus? Parents/mentors should record the experience in the Family in Faith Journal.

Fun for Review

Props: Pirate's patches for Ahab and Jezebel, paper and pen/pencil

Characters: Narrator, Naboth, Ahab, Jezebel, Elders, Nobles

Setting: NABOTH is looking over his vineyard with admiration.

NARRATOR: This is the story about a king who didn't get what he wanted … and he pitched a royal fit! *(Turning dramatically)* Now, behold Naboth admiring his vineyards!

NABOTH: Wow, these vines are awesome! And look at how healthy these grapes are! I have a wonderful vineyard. Thank You, Lord.

NARRATOR: Here comes the king.

AHAB: *(AHAB approaches NABOTH with royal pride. Speaking with a royal tone)* Behold the presence of your king, Mr. Naboth. *(NABOTH goes to his knees in reverence. AHAB holds down his hand to have NABOTH kiss his ring. NABOTH thinks AHAB is offering a hand to help him up. He takes it and rises to his feet.)*

NABOTH: Thanks, your highness. *(AHAB looks disgusted and wipes off his hand.)*

AHAB: *(Still with disgust)* Don't mention it. *(Changing tone back to royal status; clears throat)* Say, my good fellow. You have a rather awesome vineyard. I should be happy to own such a piece of land. I shall pay you handsomely for it—whatever it takes. Just give me your "yes," Naboth.

NABOTH: No, your highness.

AHAB: No, Naboth. *Yes!*

NABOTH: Yes, your highness, but *no!*

AHAB: You mean *yes.*

NABOTH: No, I mean "no." Sorry, your highness.

NARRATOR: King Ahab leaves Naboth and returns to his palace home, where his wife Jezebel is waiting.

(ELDERS and NOBLES are at the front and bow as AHAB passes into his home. AHAB acknowledges them properly, but as soon as he gets home he pitches a fit.)

JEZEBEL: Oh, hi, honey-pots! How'd it go?

AHAB: *(Stomping up and down like a spoiled child)* Oooohhh, drat! Double-drat! Mashed potatoes! *(Starting to cry)* I WANT NABOTH'S VINEYARD! I WANT IT! I WANT IT! I WANT IT!

JEZEBEL: It's okay, my little pookie-poo, kingie-wingie. If you want his vineyard, you'll get his vineyard! Now go wash up; it's almost time for dinner.

(Like a little child sulking, AHAB leaves the room.)

NARRATOR: And so the spoiled boy who would be king—I mean spoiled King Ahab—went to wash up for dinner. Meanwhile, his lovely wife—albeit a conniving wife—the first lady, Jezebel, comes up with a great, yet wicked idea.

JEZEBEL: *(Taking up paper and pen/pencil)* I have a great, yet wicked idea!

NARRATOR: She writes a letter, puts the king's official seal of approval on it, and gives it to the elders and nobles—to give to the elders and nobles in Naboth's land.

Finish the Lesson

Why does God care about our thoughts? Thoughts easily turn into actions.

What is the true source of contentment? You will find contentment in Your Lord alone. He created you for Himself.

Closing Prayer

Focus the attention of the group by reciting the Ninth and Tenth Commandments responsively (*LSCE*, p. 11). Then pray this or a similar prayer based on the commandments:

Triune God—Father, Son, and Holy Spirit—You created our hearts and minds. Teach us to fear Your wrath so we don't scheme against our neighbors. Teach us to love You so that we use our hearts and minds to encourage one another. Through Jesus, forgive us when we scheme against one another. Amen.

Lesson Suggestion

Hymn: *LW* 331:1, 10–12; *TLH* 287; *AGPS 159*

Homework: *LSCE* questions 63–68. Have students write a summary paragraph of what they learned or answer the questions in *Exploring Luther's Small Catechism,* page 19.

Memory Work: Ninth and Tenth Commandments; Matthew 15:19 (213); Psalm 37:4 (224)

11 Close of the Commandments

Focus on the Catechism

Focus the attention of the group by reciting the Close of the Commandments responsively (*LSCE,* p. 12). Then pray this or a similar prayer based on the Close of the Commandments:

Lord God, You threaten to punish all who break Your Law, yet You promise grace and every blessing to all who love You and keep Your commandments. Stir our hearts to true love and devotion this day through Christ, our Lord. Amen.

Activity

Materials: 3 to 5 belts

Strap a volunteer in a chair. You will want to use a heavy chair if possible. Use belts to secure the person in place. Strap the person's legs, arms, stomach, and thighs to the chair. This will require three to five belts. You will want to make certain that the person is not able to move. Now command the volunteer to do impossible tasks like "Scratch your forehead." After a few attempts, ask the volunteer to stop.

Say, **Watching _____ try to do what we request is like watching the result of sin and the Law. Because of sin, we are not able to keep the commandments. We are helpless.** Ask, **Which commandments have you kept perfectly?** Remind the students that if they have broken one of the commandments, God says they are guilty of breaking all the commandments. Say, **The Law doesn't help us do good; it shows us how much we need help!**

However, the Gospel tells us that God is here to save us, to set us free. Ask a volunteer to unstrap the person. Say, **This is how the Gospel works in our life. The Gospel is what God has done and continues to do for our salvation. The Gospel shows us how Jesus came to take away our sin. We would be stuck and condemned without Jesus. The Gospel sets us free from sin.**

Table Talk

(Don't just read—TELL the following true story.)

Some snickered when Willie King's doctors admitted that they had made a mistake by amputating his leg—the wrong leg. But a report from the Institute of Medicine has silenced all snickering. This report shows that more than 44,000 patients die each year from medical accidents: everyone from older patients to small children like eight-year-old Ben Kolb, who received the wrong medicine before surgery. More people die each year from medical mistakes than from car accidents, breast cancer, or AIDS. Even when doctors and nurses mean well, applying the wrong treatment can be deadly.

People also make mistakes when they apply the spiritual treatments of God's Word, the Law and the Gospel. Law and Gospel work like powerful medicines. Each has different effects, and we must apply them carefully. For example, God's Law powerfully condemns us when we don't recognize our sin. The Law drives us to repentance. But the Gospel heals us, creates in us clean hearts, and gives us new life. When people misread the Bible and mix up the treatments of Law and Gospel, the results can be spiritually deadly and damning!

Discuss one-on-one or in small groups the following questions. (Mentors will guide students through the lesson sheets.)

➡ <u>Student material starts here.</u>

Do good intentions always bring good results? Explain your answer.

No. Because we are sinners, we may try to do the right thing and still hurt ourselves or someone else.

Do doctors and nurses want to hurt or heal their patients?

Doctors and nurses don't intend to hurt their patients. Like everyone, they make mistakes.

How does God's Law work like medicine?

The Law condemns and confronts our sin, similar to how some medicines attack an illness.

How does the Gospel work like medicine?

The Gospel grants us spiritual healing and new life, similar to how some medicines grant healing.

Bible Study

In a previous lesson we read about David's sin with Bathsheba. Today's Bible story describes how the prophet Nathan confronts David with his sin. Read 2 Samuel 12:1–20.

1. What made Nathan's job difficult?

David was a strong king. He could have done away with the prophet and no one would have stopped him.

2. If you were Nathan and you had a friend who had sinned, what kind of illustration might you use to help him see his sin? Use the same format Nathan used (verses 1–4), only update it by changing the characters.

Answers will vary.

3. Name a time when you felt like David feels in verses 7–10. Did you feel frightened? ashamed? guilty?

Answers will vary.

4. Identify where the Law is forcefully proclaimed in the story.

Verses 9–10.

5. Identify how Nathan proclaims the Gospel of God's forgiveness.

Verse 13 states, "The LORD has taken away your sin."

6. How do David's actions show that he truly feared, loved, and trusted in God?

He repented when Nathan confronted him with his sin.

7. Read together Colossians 1:13–14 in celebration of the forgiveness that is yours through Jesus Christ. What part of this passage do you find most striking?

Answers will vary.

Family in Faith Journal

When parents show us our mistakes, they act like God applying His Law. When parents forgive us, they act like God applying the Gospel. Have students recall a time when their parents forgave them, recording the event in the Family in Faith Journal.

Fun for Review

Props: 3 chairs

Characters: Matchmaker, a male and a female to play Law and Gospel

Setting: TV studio

MATCHMAKER: Hi, everyone! Welcome to the show everyone is talking about—"Matches Made in Heaven." I'm the Matchmaker, and tonight we have a true match made in heaven. First, let's give a big welcome to … Law!

(Everyone claps.)

LAW: *(Enters; sits to the right of MATCHMAKER)* Thank you. It's good to be here.

MATCHMAKER: We're excited to introduce you to what should be a match made in heaven. Before we meet your match, tell us, where are you from?

LAW: I grew up on Mount Sinai. It's definitely God's country. But I was first revealed in a garden.

MATCHMAKER: I understand that now you are a world traveler?

LAW: That's correct.

MATCHMAKER: Well, you have that in common with your match made in heaven, whom we want to bring out now. Come on out, Gospel! Let's show Gospel some love by putting our hands together.

(All clap. GOSPEL enters. MATCHMAKER and LAW stand. GOSPEL sits on the other side of MATCHMAKER.)

GOSPEL: You are so gracious. Thank you.

MATCHMAKER: I understand *you* are the gracious one.

GOSPEL: Well, grace is my middle name.

LAW: You can't have a middle name if you don't have a last name.

MATCHMAKER: Good point, Law. Anyway, where are you from?

GOSPEL: I'm much older than I look. I'm eternal. I was first announced as a promise to a couple named Adam and Eve.

MATCHMAKER: And since then you've been carried into the world, correct?

GOSPEL: That's right. I use my gifts wherever I'm proclaimed. It keeps me busy, but I love what I do.

MATCHMAKER: Let's learn a little about what each of you do for a living. Law, let's start with you.

LAW: I show people their sins. I set down rules and guidelines. I look them in the eyes and show them where they have failed. Part of my time is also spent acting as a kind of curb so people aren't doing whatever they want to do. In addition, I guide believers in the way they are to live as God's forgiven people in Christ.

MATCHMAKER: That job must keep you busy! *(LAW nods.)* So, Gospel, tell us what you do.

GOSPEL: My name means "Good News," and that tells my work. I love bringing the Good News to people who have met up with Law. You see, Law, you may not have realized it, but I've been following you around for a long time.

LAW: What? Really?

GOSPEL: You show people their sins, and I show them their Savior. I get to tell them that there is hope through the forgiveness of their sins. Jesus came to die for them and to save them from their sins. I share Jesus' love, His promises, and all of His Good News.

LAW: I thought that since we were total opposites, we'd never be a match, but it's just the opposite.

MATCHMAKER: You need each other. Without Law there would be no need for Gospel. And who would need to hear the Gospel's message if they didn't know Law? This truly is a match made in heaven! Well, that's our show for tonight!

Finish the Lesson

How do Law and Gospel go well together? Both messages come from God and are designed to work together for our good.

Why should the Gospel follow the Law? The Law can't save. It shows us our sin. However, the Gospel saves us from the condemnation of the Law.

Closing Prayer

Focus the attention of the group by reciting the Close of the Commandments responsively (*LSCE,* p. 12). Then pray this or a similar prayer based on the Close of the Commandments:

Lord God, You threaten to punish all who break Your Law, yet You promise grace and every blessing to all who love You and keep Your commandments. Forgive us when we fail to heed Your Law. Through the Gospel, stir our hearts to true love and devotion this day; through Christ, our Lord. Amen.

Lesson Suggestions

Hymn: *LW* 355; *TLH* 377; *AGPS* 230

Homework: *LSCE* questions 69–73. Have students write a summary paragraph of what they learned or answer the questions in *Exploring Luther's Small Catechism,* pages 21–22.

Memory Work: Close of the Commandments; Psalm 5:4–5 (227); John 3:16 (270)

12 Table of Duties, Calling throughout Life

Focus on the Catechism

Focus the attention of the group by reciting "To Youth" through "To Everyone" responsively (*LSCE*, pp. 37–38). Then pray the following prayer based on the Table of Duties:

Heavenly Father, whether we are young or old, You call us to humbly walk before You and call others to faith in Jesus Christ. Help us to love others this day even as we love ourselves. To Your name be all glory, forever and ever. Amen.

Activity

Materials: Red construction paper, black markers, scissors, safety pins

Have students trace and cut out a copy of the two tablets of the Law. Use black markers to write in the two tables of the Law: commandments 1–3 on the first tablet and 4–10 on the second. Cross the tablets to form the shape of a heart.

Say, **In the Table of Duties we learn the heart of the Ten Commandments.** Read Romans 13:9. **The Ten Commandments are all about love, love for God and for one another. God calls us and commands us to love one another as we love ourselves.**

Have students pin their commandment-hearts on each other.

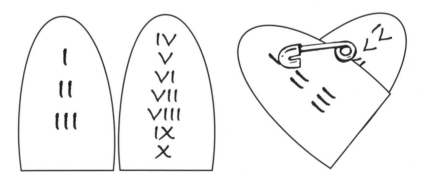

Table Talk

You have heard numerous stories in class. Now break into small groups or one-on-one. With the help of the parents/mentors, have students write the story of their life with God. Include the effects of God's Law and Gospel on their lives. Share some of the stories with the group.

Examine the passages under "To Youth," "To Widows," and "To Everyone" (*LSCE*, pp. 37–38).

➡ Student material starts here.

As Romans 13:9 shows, love for our neighbor is always based on God's love for our neighbors. According to 2 Peter 3:9, what does God desire for your neighbors?

God is lovingly patient and wants everyone to repent.

Bible Study

Everywhere Jesus looked, He saw men and women who were "like sheep without a shepherd" (Matthew 9:36). Determined to multiply His ministry, He sent His disciples out to help with the work. He warned that the work of discipleship would often meet with resistance, even from within one's own family. Read Matthew 9:35–38 and 10:37–42.

1. If Jesus asked you to help Him care for other people, how might you respond?

Answers will vary.

2. How might your response change in view of Matthew 10:37–39?

Hopefully students will want to help spread the Gospel.

3. What does "taking up the cross" (Matthew 10:38) indicate might happen as we carry out our God-given purpose in life?

We will suffer and face persecution.

4. If a leader at your church encouraged you to become a pastor, deaconess, director of Christian education, teacher, or missionary, what might you say?

Answers will vary. Not everyone can or should become a full-time church worker. However, students should carefully consider God's calling for their lives.

5. In what way is Matthew 9:37–38 as true today as it was when Jesus spoke the words?

There is a shortage of church workers.

6. Do you have to be a trained church worker to share God's Word with others?

No. Sunday School teachers and the like share God's Word.

7. Discuss with your parent/mentor his or her job. How does this job show love and care for other people?

Answers will vary.

8. Point out where the story proclaims the Law and the Gospel.

For example, verse 10:37 strongly proclaims the Law. Verses 9:35–36 describe Jesus' ministry of mercy.

9. What was Jesus' calling and what does it mean for your life?

The heavenly Father called Jesus to give His life as the Savior of the world. He has taken away my sins.

Family in Faith Journal

Though Christians have individual callings as parents or children, we all have a common calling according to Romans 13:9 and 1 Timothy 2:1. From these two verses, have students write God's common calling for their life in their Family in Faith Journal.

Fun for Review

Prop: Phone (if not available, pantomime)

Characters: Sarah, Voice of Jesus (over the phone)

Setting: Sarah's home

(Sound of phone ringing)

SARAH: *(Answering phone)* Hello?

JESUS: Sarah, how are you?

SARAH: Jesus—it's You!

JESUS: You know My voice. I wrote in My book that My sheep—My children—know My voice.

SARAH: And You called me by name.

JESUS: You are mine, Sarah. You are My child, whom I love.

SARAH: I love You too, Jesus.

JESUS: Did you enjoy the day I shared with you today?

SARAH: It was great, thanks. Great job on the sunset! And thanks for Your help on the history test.

JESUS: I'm pretty good with history, aren't I?

SARAH: By the way, is this a long distance call?

JESUS: It is long distance; well, actually, it's about a long distance call.

SARAH: I haven't made any long distance calls lately.

JESUS: I'm not talking about a phone call.

SARAH: You're confusing me, Jesus.

JESUS: I wanted to remind you about the long distance call you have, Sarah.

SARAH: This one?

JESUS: Remember, it's not a phone call … it's about My calling you to stick with Me for the long haul. I'm sticking with you, Sarah. I will always be there for you and I have great plans for you.

SARAH: So You're talking about the idea of You calling me to be Your child for a long distance—through this earthly life and into heaven one day.

JESUS: You've got the idea!

SARAH: Sometimes I think I'm not all that important, Jesus. I'm sorry for that.

JESUS: You're forgiven! You're special!

SARAH: And You want to use me somehow?

JESUS: There are lots of people that will be coming in and out of your life that don't know about Me. I want you to tell them about Me.

SARAH: But I'm always afraid I'll say the wrong thing.

JESUS: I'm going to give you the words to say. Remember that little girl you helped on the playground last week? You were great with her.

SARAH: I never imagined that You were behind that. I *did* know what to say and do. You're awesome!

JESUS: So are you!

SARAH: Thanks for calling me today and thanks for calling me through Baptism. You have given me a real long distance call. With Your help, I'll make it to the end!

JESUS: Sounds like a great plan. You can count on Me. Don't be afraid to tell others about Me. Use the phone if you want. You're very comfortable talking on the phone.

SARAH: That's what all my friends say! Thanks! You're a great problem solver in more ways than one! Should I say good-bye or Amen?

JESUS: Let's just keep talking … phone or no phone. Remember, this is a long distance call without long distance charges!

Finish the Lesson

How important are you to Jesus? How do you know? So important that He gave His life for me on the cross.

With a partner, practice telling someone else why Jesus is important for you and your life. Responses will vary.

Closing Prayer

Focus the attention of the group by reciting "To Youth" through "To Everyone" responsively (*LSCE,* pp. 37–38). Then pray the following prayer based on the Table of Duties.

Heavenly Father, whether we are young or old, You call us to humbly walk before You and call others to faith in Jesus Christ. Forgive us when we fail to bear witness to Your wonderful gift of salvation. Help us to love others this day even as we love ourselves. To Your name be all glory, forever and ever. Amen.

Lesson Suggestions

Hymn: *LW* 314; *TLH* 512; *AGPS* 171

Homework: *LSCE* questions 78–85. Have students write a summary paragraph of what they learned or answer the questions in *Exploring Luther's Small Catechism,* page 22.

Memory Work: Romans 13:9 (p. 37); 1 Timothy 2:1 (p. 38)

Special Projects: Invite your congregation's evangelism director to describe the various outreach efforts of the congregation; arrange for students to receive evangelism experience with an organization such as Ongoing Ambassadors for Christ.

Prayer upon Completing Study of the Ten Commandments

Following the sermon, the confirmands and their parents/mentors shall come forward. They shall face the congregation, confirmands in front; parents/mentors behind. Then the minister shall say:

Beloved in the Lord, after receiving the Ten Commandments from God's hand, the prophet Moses said to the parents of Israel: "These commandments that I give you today are to be upon your hearts. Impress them on your children. Talk about them when you sit at home and when you walk along the road, when you lie down and when you get up."

The students shall then speak together the Ten Commandments.

Let us pray for our catechumens, that our Lord God would open their hearts and the door of His mercy that they may remain faithful to Christ Jesus, our Lord:

Almighty God and Father, because You always grant growth to Your Church, increase the faith and understanding of our catechumens that, recalling the new birth by the water of Holy Baptism, they may forever continue in the family of those whom You adopt as Your sons and daughters; through Jesus Christ, our Lord.

Response: Amen.

Adapted from *Lutheran Worship*, pp. 205, 276.

13

Apostles' Creed,
First Article A

Focus on the Catechism

Focus the attention of the group by reciting the First Article responsively (*LSCE,* pp. 13–14). Then pray this or a similar prayer based on the First Article:

We praise You, dear Father, that You care for us daily, richly providing us with everything we need. Defend us against all danger this day so that we might thank and praise, serve and obey You through Christ, our Lord. Amen.

Activity

Materials: Flower or vegetable seeds, pot, potting soil, fertilizer, water

Tell the students that you want to grow some plants, and then throw some seeds on a desk or table. Then walk away. Ask, **Will these seeds grow? Why?** (Students should mention that you need to do more than throw some seeds on a desk if you want plants to grow.) Show them a pot, some soil, fertilizer, and water. Have students plant the seeds properly. Say, **Just as seeds require continuous care, you need the loving care of your Creator each day. God has not created you and then thrown you out on your own.**

Ask, **What specific things does God give you to care for your daily needs? In what specific ways can you thank Him for His fatherly kindness and care?** Say, **This part of the Apostles' Creed can remind you that God provides everything you need from day to day. He gives you forgiveness, life, and salvation in Jesus, along with temporal blessings. He does this because He is your loving, heavenly Father.**

Table Talk

(Don't just read—TELL the following true story.)

In 1554 a scientist in Poland published a discovery that revolutionized our understanding of the world. He proved that the earth is not the center of the universe, but actually revolves around the sun. His book *On the Revolutions of the Celestial Spheres* was so controversial that it was banned by the Roman Catholic Church.

Today, many scientists point to the banning of this book and claim that this proves Christians cannot be good scientists. They argue that because Christians believe in God as the Creator of heaven and earth, that belief will prevent them from studying the universe in a scientific way. However, the foolishness of this idea is shown by the author of the book that was banned. His name was Nicolaus Copernicus, a devout Lutheran Christian!

Some people misunderstood Copernicus's book to mean that since the earth was not the center of the universe, God was not the center of the universe. But Copernicus understood that the center of the universe was not discovered on a map of the stars. He understood that God our Creator is present everywhere. He daily and richly provides for His creation from one end of the universe to the other.

Discuss one-on-one or in small groups the following questions. (Mentors will guide students through the lesson sheets.)

➡ <u>Student material starts here.</u>

Based on the story of Copernicus, can Christians be good scientists? Explain your answer.

Yes. Scientists simply observe the creation and report what they see. When scientists build theories upon theories, they cease to be scientists.

Are scientists always right? Give examples.

No. Answers will vary.

Science is based on observing facts and reporting those facts. Who observed the origins of the universe? Only God.

The human brain has 30 billion nerve cells. In order for you to sit here today, billions of these cells must work with other cells with exact timing. Your brain sends out messages to over 200 muscles just for you to sit down. How could this happen by mere accident, or chance, as the evolutionists suggest?

It couldn't. Creation is designed by God.

Bible Study

After Jesus grows up, God calls John the Baptist to prepare the way for Jesus' ministry of salvation. Read Matthew 3.

1. If God created a perfect world, then why did people need John the Baptist's ministry of repentance?

All people have sinned and need God's forgiveness; therefore, John told people to repent.

2. Briefly describe John's preaching. What does it tell you about how the Creator feels about His creation?

God is angry about man's sin and the destruction it causes.

3. What happened when Jesus was baptized?

The heavens opened, the Spirit descended as a dove, and God spoke.

4. What three divine persons were heard or seen at Jesus' Baptism?

The Father, Son, and Holy Spirit.

5. The word "trinity" or "triune" means three (tri-) in one (-une). How does this story reveal God's threefold nature?

The Father is God. The Son is God. And the Spirit is God. These are the three persons of the Trinity.

6. How does this story reveal the Creator's power over creation? His love for creation?

God opens the heavens and the Holy Spirit assumes the bodily form of a dove (see also Luke 3:22). The heavenly Father sent His Son as the Savior of the world.

7. Contrast John's preaching with the heavenly Father's words in 3:17. How do these passages show the Law and Gospel character of God?

John's preaching proclaims God's wrath against sin. The heavenly Father is pleased with His Son's work of salvation for you.

Family in Faith Journal

Follow the teacher on a tour of the sanctuary and identify as many symbols of the Trinity as you can find. Have students choose their favorite and sketch it in the Family in Faith Journal.

Fun for Review

Characters: Bobby, Billy, Amy, Suzy, various people to make background animal noises

Setting: Zoo

(Zoo noises are heard, but die off when dialogue begins.)

BOBBY: Look at these animals!

BILLY: *(Mockingly)* Oooh! Animals. I'm so impressed!

AMY: Oh, Billy! Don't be such a cynic!

BOBBY: A what?

SUZY: She means someone who doesn't appreciate God's creation … or everything that He provides for us.

BOBBY: Look at all of the different kinds of animals! God is so amazing!

(An animal noise is made as each animal is named.)

AMY: Look, a Clydesdale horse!

SUZY: Sheep!

BOBBY: An elephant!

BILLY: Okay, I guess I like that rattlesnake over there.

AMY: Hey, a gazelle!

SUZY: Hmmm, I never knew a gazelle made a noise like that.

BILLY: And you guys think God made these animals? I think they're all products of an evolutionary process that probably started on the Galapagos Islands about a *billion* years ago.

AMY: Oh, Billy, Billy, Billy. You can't possibly tell me you believe that all of this is just some quirk of nature?

(A duck quacks.)

BILLY: She said, "QUIRK"! *(The duck quacks again.)*

SUZY: And where do you think *we* came from, Billy?

BILLY: See that ring-tailed monkey over there? *(A monkey sounds.)*

BOBBY: Oh, come on, strong-willed Bill. You've said it in church and probably never even thought about what you were saying.

BILLY: Said what?

BOBBY: What do you think it means when we confess, "I believe in God, the Father Almighty, *MAKER* of heaven and earth"?

BILLY: There you go bringing God into the picture again. Keep it for Sunday, boys and girls.

SUZY: How can you look at this world and not think of Almighty God? I see beautiful mountains or a magnificent sunset and I say, "Thank You, Lord."

AMY: I see these animals and think to myself, "Wow, Lord! You've made some amazing creatures."

(All animal sounds chime in.)

BOBBY: I look at us! Everything God has blessed us with: our clothes, food, and, dare I say, even our parents?

AMY: Everything we need to support this life comes from God.

BILLY: Oh yeah? Well, I see a broken world—and animals that bite …

(Something growls. They all simultaneously take one step backward.)

BILLY: What did this poor loser of a world do to deserve all of this?

BOBBY: Actually a lot.

AMY and SUZY: Sin!

BILLY: Then why would God still provide all of those so-called beautiful things? What'd we do to deserve *that*?

BOBBY: Not a thing, bub.

AMY: Nope. Nothin'.

SUZY: It's called love.

BOBBY: It's called grace.

AMY: Admit it, Billy-boy, you've got a lot to be thankful for.

BILLY: Yeah, yeah. I suppose.

BOBBY: Hey, guys! Let's go look at that gazelle again. I think he's finally cleared his throat.

Finish the Lesson

How does the beauty and complexity of creation point to God? This simply could not happen by chance. The world has an obvious design.

Why might the theory of evolution attract some people? Some people crave an explanation of life that does not include God. They understand that if they believe in God, they must listen to what God has to say about their lives.

Closing Prayer

Focus the attention of the group by reciting the First Article responsively (*LSCE,* pp. 13–14). Then pray this or a similar prayer based on the First Article:

We praise You, dear Father, that You care for us daily, richly providing us with everything we need. Defend us against all danger this day so that we might thank and praise, serve and obey You through Christ, our Lord. Amen.

Lesson Suggestions

Hymn: *LW* 212 or 213; *TLH* 251 or 252; *AGPS* 136

Homework: *LSCE* questions 94–100. Have students write a summary paragraph of what they learned or answer the questions in *Exploring Luther's Small Catechism,* page 25, sections A and C.

Memory Work: First Article (through "still takes care of them"); Malachi 2:10 (321); Colossians 1:16 (328)

14

Apostles' Creed, First Article B

Focus on the Catechism

Focus the attention of the group by reciting the First Article responsively (*LSCE,* pp. 13-14). Then pray this or a similar prayer based on the First Article:

We praise You, Father Almighty, that You sustain our lives each day by richly providing all we need. Help us to care for Your creation, to love and respect all You have made; through Jesus Christ, our Lord. Amen.

Activity

Materials: Candle and candleholder, matches, oscillating fan, plastic bottle

Ask a student to light the candle and place it in the holder. Bring out an oscillating fan. Ask the students what the fan might do to the candle. A strong gust of wind and the flame will be blown out.

Turn on the fan and let it rotate around. Eventually the wind will blow out the candle. Tell the class the flame was helpless. There was nothing it could do to defend itself. Say, **The candle can remind us of ourselves without God. We are defenseless against the evil in the world, against Satan, against sin, and against death. However, in the creed we learn that God protects and sustains us.** Relight the candle. Now place the plastic bottle over the candle. Turn the fan on. Again it will blow, but this time the candle will remain lit. Say, **The clear plastic covering reminds us of God's protection. We may not always be aware of God's presence, but He is all around us, defending us and all His world against all dangers and evils.** Ask students to offer suggestions of ways God sustains, protects, and defends us. List the suggestions on the board. Be sure to include the sustaining power of forgiveness in Christ.

Table Talk

(Don't just read—TELL the following true story.)

In May 1876 an Australian woman named Truganini suffered a massive stroke. Before she died, her last request to her doctors was, "Don't let them cut me up." But the doctors didn't listen. Rather than leave her body in a cemetery, they scraped away Truganini's flesh, boiled her bones, and then put them in a glass display case at the Hobart Museum. For years, people visited the museum to see Truganini's bones. Why? Because she was the last member of an extinct tribe of people, the last Tasmanian Aborigine.

During the 1800s and 1900s European and American scientists harvested the corpses of Australian Aborigines, Africans, and other races of people. The theory of evolution had convinced these scientists that some races were not fully human. Therefore, many scientists concluded that they could analyze people like animals. Thousands became specimens for the evolutionists' so-called "scientific" research.

Discuss one-on-one or in small groups the following questions. (Mentors will guide students through the lesson sheets.)

➡ Student material starts here.

How is the theory of evolution a dangerous teaching?

Evolution has caused many people to treat other people like animals. They don't respect God's gift of life.

Do you have to believe in evolution to be a good scientist? Defend your answer.

No. Good science is based on observation, not evolutionary theory.

How does your belief in God affect the way you see other people?

God's Spirit moves God's children to respect the gift of life that God has given to others.

If God is almighty, why do you think some people have a hard time believing that He simply created everything out of nothing through His Word?

Many scientists say that they reject any belief based on faith. Yet these same scientists trust in evolutionary theories that are based on faith in theories instead of observation.

Bible Study

After creating the earth, God personally creates the first people. Read Genesis 2.

1. In your own words, describe the Garden of Eden before humankind sinned.

Students should note that creation was perfect and harmonious.

2. Why are you glad God did something about man's loneliness? See 2:18–23.

When God created Eve, He created the family.

3. What do you think God meant when He said the woman would be a "helper"?

The word "helper" also means "ally." Although God created Adam and Eve to be different, they are equally human.

4. Explain why Adam and Eve didn't wear clothes and yet were not ashamed. Contrast that scene to what it says in Genesis 3:10. What happened that brought about shame?

At first, Adam and Eve had no sin. They had no evil thoughts, but respected each other. After disobeying God by eating the forbidden fruit, they lost respect for each other.

5. After Adam and Eve listened to Satan and rebelled, how did God promise to save them? See 3:15.

God promised the birth of a Savior who would defeat the devil. This is the first promise about Jesus.

6. Point out where the story proclaims the Law and the Gospel.

For example, verses 2:15–17 strongly proclaim the Law. Genesis 2:7 points forward to the new life God gives in the Gospel.

Family in Faith Journal

Parents/mentors should describe the wonder of a child's birth. If possible, have parents tell the students about their own birth and how they regard the child as a gift of God. Students should record this in the Family in Faith Journal.

Fun for Review

Prop: Sunglasses (if available)

Characters: Host, Heckler, Inventor 1 (male), Inventor 2 (female—wearing sunglasses), Inventor 3 (male), Judge

Setting: A convention center

HOST: Welcome to the impressively important inaugural International Invention Institution in Indianapolis, Indiana.

HECKLER: *(Offstage)* We can't hear you! And could you talk a little faster?

HOST: *(Faster and louder)* Welcome to the impressively important inaugural International Invention Institution in Indianapolis, Indiana.

HECKLER: Easy for you to say!

HOST: We have three finalists. Awards for these inventions will be based on creativity, usefulness, and lasting quality of workmanship.

HECKLER: Did anyone create a belly-button-lint remover?

HOST: No! Our first inventor made something that he couldn't actually bring in today. So if you'll take a look at the video screen, he'll tell you about his creation.

INVENTOR 1: Thank you. I made a mountain out of a molehill. As you can see on the screen, I began with a molehill approximately one foot high. I chased the mole out so he wouldn't get hurt. Then I accumulated dirt, dust-bunnies, trash, and other material I found under my teenager's bed. I eventually created this immovable mountain that stands at 5,230 feet above sea level. Thank you.

HOST: Let's give inventor number 1 a big hand.

(All clap.)

HOST: Without further ado, let's bring up our second finalist.

INVENTOR 2: *(Pretending to roll a large, bright ball)* Hello! Sorry for the bright light. In fact, you may want to shade your eyes. I created a star. It started as a light bulb. I looked at the bulb and said, "Baby, you're going to be a star one day!"

HOST: Let's give a big hand for our second inventor while welcoming our last inventor.

(All clap.)

INVENTOR 3: I'm really embarrassed. I had a little problem coming to the convention hall today. I had created the perfect being. It had no fears and no shame, it never sinned, it always picked up its clothes, and it couldn't die. But I just found out that it could break. On the way here, it fell and broke. My original masterpiece isn't like it used to be. I couldn't even save it. Thanks for your time.

HOST: The judges are tallying their votes. *(Receives an envelope from JUDGE)* Ladies and gentlemen, I have the final vote. *(Opens envelope)* Oh, no! There's a problem. Our judges have disqualified all our contestants because their work isn't original. Here's a judge to explain.

JUDGE: It's obvious that each inventor stole his or her ideas from the greatest creator ever—God. God created the mountains, the stars, and the whole universe. And as for the perfect human being … hello? Has anyone read Genesis? Perfect humans, the fall, things aren't the same? The only thing different is that God *was* able to save His fallen creation through His Son, Jesus. This competition is a farce! Let's give God a hand for His creative work all around us!

(All clap.)

Finish the Lesson

How does God's creativity differ from ours? God created all things out of nothing through His Word. Ever since, we have been creative by simply altering what God already made.

How might the fact that God created you give you confidence for life? God knows how my life should work. He guides my life through His Word.

Closing Prayer

Focus the attention of the group by reciting the First Article responsively (*LSCE,* p. 13–14). Then pray this or a similar prayer based on the First Article:

We praise You, Father Almighty, that You sustain our lives each day by richly providing all we need. Forgive us when we doubt Your care. Help us to care for Your creation, to love and respect all You have made; through Jesus Christ, our Lord. Amen.

Lesson Suggestions

Hymn: *LW* 210; *TLH* 238; *AGPS* 257

Homework: *LSCE* questions 101–113. Have students write a summary paragraph of what they learned or answer the questions in *Exploring Luther's Small Catechism,* page 25, section B, and pages 26–27.

Memory Work: First Article ("He also gives ... most certainly true"); Jeremiah 1:5 (346); Colossians 1:17 (363)

15

Apostles' Creed, Second Article A

Focus on the Catechism

Focus the attention of the group by reciting the Second Article responsively (*LSCE*, p. 14). Then pray this or a similar prayer based on the Second Article:

We praise You, Lord Jesus Christ, that even though You are God, You were born of the Virgin Mary so that You could redeem us from all sins. Strengthen us this day to live as servants of Your heavenly Father. Through Your merits we pray. Amen.

Activity

Materials: Iron, squirt bottle filled with water

Ask, **What's an iron made of?** (Iron!) Now turn on the iron. Say, **When I turn on this iron, what happens to the metal it's made of?** (It heats up.) **Is it still metal?** (Yes. The heat changes the iron, but it's still metal.) **How can we tell the iron isn't just metal but also has heat?** Students should note the spray bottle. Allow a student to spray some water on the iron. Say, **If you just look at an iron, you can't really tell if it's just metal or if it's heated metal, if something is present that you can't see.**

These facts about an iron can help us understand Jesus. When people looked at Jesus, what do you think they saw? (A man.) **Could they tell whether Jesus was also God just by looking at Him?** (No. But Jesus' actions, His miracles, showed that He was different from an ordinary man.) **Today we're going to learn that Jesus was more than an ordinary man. He was God and man in one person.**

Table Talk

(Don't just read—TELL the following true story.)

In the early centuries of the church, a false teacher named Arius arose who claimed that Jesus wasn't truly God. Arius confused many people. When they read the Bible, they saw passages that seemed to teach that Jesus was an ordinary man. But they also read other passages that seemed to teach that Jesus was eternal, almighty God. In their confusion they turned to Pastor Augustine for help, asking, "Could Jesus be both God and man?"

Pastor Augustine helped them understand who Jesus was with an illustration. He noted that when you put a piece of iron into a fire, it heats up until it glows red hot. The iron remains iron and the fire remains fire. But the two have become one. Augustine explained that it works the same way with our Lord. Just as the iron is still iron and the fire is still fire even though they are joined together, Jesus is still a man and He is still God even though God and man have come together in Him. For our salvation, God and man joined together in the one person of Jesus Christ.

Discuss one-on-one or in small groups the following questions. (Mentors will guide students through the lesson sheets.)

➡ <u>Student material starts here.</u>

Consider for a moment how God created the world, raised the dead, and was born of a virgin. How is it possible for Him to be both God and man?

He's God! He has miraculous power.

How is the Bible's teaching that Jesus is true man a comfort to you?

He can understand me and my personal struggles because He has experienced them.

Cults like the Mormons and the Jehovah's Witnesses don't believe that Jesus is truly God. Why is that important?

They contradict the Bible and don't really understand Jesus. They don't understand that He is the only Savior and we cannot save ourselves. They don't understand that if Jesus isn't God, He cannot be the Savior!

Bible Study

After hours of teaching and ministering to crowds of people, Jesus and His disciples sail across the Sea of Galilee. Read Mark 4:35–41.

1. Which part of the story shows that Jesus was human? Which part shows He was divine?

He fell asleep. He stilled the storm with a word.

2. How do you think the disciples felt before and after the storm?

Fearful before, fearful and surprised after!

3. Name a time when you felt as the disciples must have felt before Jesus awoke.

Answers will vary.

4. Name a time when you felt like the disciples must have felt after Jesus stilled the storm.

Answers will vary. Students may recall a time when God protected them.

5. What does Jesus' name literally mean? In your own words, tell another person how Jesus saved you.

Jesus means, "Yahweh (LORD) saves." Students should witness that Jesus saved them by keeping the Law for them, by dying for them on the cross, and by rising from the dead.

6. In your own words, tell one another what it means to say, "I believe in Jesus Christ."

To believe in Jesus means to trust that He can and does save us from our sins.

7. What do you confess about Jesus' conception and birth according to the Apostles' Creed?

Jesus became a human being so that He could save me and all other people.

Family in Faith Journal

Parents/mentors should describe how they first learned about Jesus and how their understanding has changed over time. Have students record these memories in the Family in Faith Journal.

Fun for Review

Props: Chairs—to be arranged as seating in a boat with three chairs set up for Jesus to sleep on and a chair for Disciple 1 in front of everyone else's, like a captain's chair on a bridge; cushion or pillow

Characters: 6 Disciples, Jesus Christ

Setting: JESUS and the DISCIPLES are walking to the boat. JESUS is just finishing up explaining a parable.

DISCIPLES 3–6: TO THE OTHER SIDE!

DISCIPLE 1: *(Pointing ahead)* Engage!

DISCIPLE 2: Aye, aye, captain!

DISCIPLE 6: Do y'all see what I see?

DISCIPLES: *(With combined panic)* Yeah, we do.

DISCIPLE 1: Great! This is just great! Someone wake the Master.

DISCIPLE 2: Aye, captain, but He did say He needed some rest.

(DISCIPLES mimic a fierce storm [i.e., swaying back and forth].)

DISCIPLE 3: Oh, the wind!

DISCIPLE 4: Oh, the rain!

DISCIPLE 5: Oh, the waves!

DISCIPLE 6: Oh, I think I'm gonna be sick!

(With even greater panic)

DISCIPLE 2: Captain! She's breaking up! She's breaking up!

DISCIPLE 1: More power! We need more power!

DISCIPLE 3–6: WE-ARE-GOING-TO-DIE!

(Continue to make commotion and fierce storm sounds or whatever.)

DISCIPLE 1: Somebody! Somebody get to Jesus! Wake Him! Do it now!

DISCIPLE 2: Aye, captain! I think I can make it to the stern!

DISCIPLE 1: And quit saying, "Aye, captain"!

DISCIPLE 2: Aye, captain! I … I mean, sure! You got it, baby!

(DISCIPLE 2 makes his way to JESUS and shakes Him awake.)

DISCIPLE 2: Wake up! PLEASE wake up! Teacher, don't you care if we drown?

(JESUS gets up and walks to the center of the boat. He's walking normally.)

DISCIPLE 3: Oh, the wind!

DISCIPLE 4: Oh, the rain!

DISCIPLE 5: Oh, the waves!

DISCIPLE 6: Oh, I think I'm gonna be sick!

JESUS: Oh, be quiet! Be still!

(Everything is calm. The DISCIPLES sit down. JESUS remains standing with arms folded, looking at the DISCIPLES.)

JESUS: Why are you so afraid? Do you still have no faith?

(The DISCIPLES are trembling, yet relieved.)

DISCIPLE 2: Aye, Sir. We were very afraid.

DISCIPLES 3–6: Thank You, Teacher.

(JESUS goes back to the stern and lies down.)

(DISCIPLE 2 raising an eyebrow and standing next to DISCIPLE 1 at his chair)

DISCIPLE 2: Most curious, captain.

DISCIPLE 1: Agreed. He's just as human as we are, but only God has that kind of authority over the wind and the waves. Curious, indeed.

(DISCIPLES 3-6 talk among themselves.)

Finish the Lesson

What connection do you see between the confession that God created heaven and earth and this miracle of Jesus? Jesus is truly God and displays His mighty power.

Why might God permit natural disasters? Since the fall, sin has corrupted and distorted the natural world. This led to "natural" disasters. God permits such disasters so that we might know the consequences of our sin and repent.

Closing Prayer

Focus the attention of the group by reciting the Second Article responsively (*LSCE,* p. 14). Then pray this or a similar prayer based on the Second Article:

We praise You, Lord Jesus Christ, that even though You are God, You were born of the Virgin Mary so that You could redeem us from all sins. Strengthen us this day to live as servants of Your heavenly Father. Forgive our doubts. Through Your merits we pray. Amen.

Lesson Suggestions

Hymn: *LW* 212 or 213; *TLH* 251 or 252; *AGPS* 217

Homework: *LSCE* questions 114–124. Have students answer questions in *Exploring Luther's Small Catechism*, pages 13–14, or have students write a summary of what they have learned.

Memory Work: Second Article (through "is my Lord"); John 1:1–2 (390); 1 Timothy 2:5 (401)

16

Apostles' Creed, Second Article B

Focus on the Catechism

Focus the attention of the group by reciting the Second Article responsively (*LSCE*, p. 14). Then pray this or a similar prayer based on the Second Article:

We praise You, Lord Jesus Christ, that with Your holy, precious blood and with Your innocent suffering and death, You purchased and won life for us. Help us to live each day to Your glory. In Your holy name we pray. Amen.

Activity

Say, **You have just learned that your son or daughter is terminally ill. Your child needs an organ transplant in order to survive. The doctors have run various tests and found that you (the parent) are the perfect donor. Your child will live if you donate the organ, but the operation will kill you.**

Now ask the parents one by one whether they would donate the organ. Then ask why. (They will respond with something like, "Because it's my child.")

Have the parents face their children, hold their hands, and say, "I would give my life for you because you are my own son/daughter."

Explain, **Today we learn about the amazing love and self-sacrifice Jesus made for us so that we might be His own and live with Him in His kingdom.**

Table Talk

(Don't just read—TELL the following true story.)

No one knew the man's name. But on January 13, 1982, he gave an unforgettable gift to four strangers who flew with him on Air Florida Flight 90.

As the plane lifted off that afternoon, ice choked its engines and caused it to crash on a bridge over the Potomac River. Freezing water swallowed up all but the tail section of the plane. Five battered souls reached the water's surface and gripped the wreckage with numb fingers.

When an emergency helicopter arrived, it dropped a rescue line to the stranded passengers. One man—described as looking about 50 years old and having a mustache—grabbed hold of the line and began passing it to the people stranded with him. The helicopter lifted the victims one at a time and hurried them to shore. Each time the helicopter reached the survivors, this mysterious man took hold of the rescue line and passed it to someone else. Four people rode to safety that night. But when the helicopter returned the last time for the unnamed man who had aided his fellow passengers, he was gone. The cold had overwhelmed him. He had slipped away beneath the waters.

Discuss one-on-one or in small groups the following questions. (Mentors will guide students through the lesson sheets.)

➡ Student material starts here.

What is most remarkable about this true story? This man sacrificed his life to save others.

How are the actions of this man similar to the actions of Jesus on the cross? How are they different? Jesus also died to save us, but His sacrifice saves us eternally from death and hell.

If you were on the tail of the plane that night and this mystery man handed you the rescue line, what might you think or say? Thank you!

How might that affect your life? Answers will vary.

Bible Study

The story of Jesus' crucifixion is a picture of a true hero. Jesus sacrificially chooses to die. He courageously suffers, dying for the sins of all humankind in order to rescue us from the consequences of sin. Read Luke 23:26–47.

1. **In this story, how are Jesus' actions heroic?** He sacrifices His life for us when He could have spared Himself.

2. **Count the number of times the word "save" appears. Define the word "save." Why is it appropriate to use this word when talking about Jesus?** Save appears three times and means "rescue." Jesus rescues us from sin, death, and the dominion of the devil.

3. **How is Jesus your personal Savior?** He surely gave His life for me and my sins.

4. **What attitude does Jesus have toward the crowd? the soldiers? the criminals?** Jesus speaks gently to the crowds, forgives the soldiers, and promises paradise.

5. **What truth about Jesus does the criminal notice in 23:41?** He has done nothing wrong. Christ kept God's Law perfectly.

6. **Point out where the story proclaims the Law and the Gospel.** For example, verses 23:28–31 strongly proclaim the Law. Luke 23:34, 43 gently proclaims the Gospel.

Family in Faith Journal

With the students, write a prayer of thanksgiving to Jesus for His personal sacrifice for us. Record it in the Family in Faith Journal.

Fun for Review

Characters: Teacher, 6 Students (S1 through S6)

Setting: Classroom. TEACHER is in front of the class. STUDENTS sit in their seats.

TEACHER: Class, today we're going to talk about Jesus' work.

S1: That's an easy subject. Jesus worked with wood and nails. He made things. You know, what's that called?

S2: A carpenter, brains!

S1: Oh, yeah. A carpenter.

S3: That was Jesus' dad, Joseph, who was the carpenter.

S1: But in those days, sons usually learned the work of their father. So He probably worked with wood and nails and stuff.

S2: Jesus worked as a teacher.

TEACHER: Tell me more about that.

S2: I think He probably taught people the most important lesson about working on a computer.

S1: What? Computer? They didn't have computers back then. They used something called typewriters.

S3: You've lost me.

S2: I figure Jesus was a computer teacher. He taught people the most important lesson: save your computer documents so they don't get lost. You've heard the news … "Jesus saves!"

S3: If you go that route, you might think Jesus worked on a Coast Guard ship. When people were drowning, He'd throw one of those doughnut-shaped things to them. He was a life savior.

S4: That's "lifesaver," dingy! Didn't He work as a doctor? He healed a bunch of people.

TEACHER: He did heal many people, but He wasn't a doctor.

S5: I thought Jesus must work in a cemetery because it seemed like that's where He really came to life. He loved His work there.

S6: My mom always says that Jesus knows the work of a mother because He was always making sacrifices for others.

TEACHER: Despite all your wild answers, your first guess was right, in a way. Jesus did work with wood and nails.

S1: See, I told you.

TEACHER: Jesus' greatest work was done when He was nailed to the cross—made of wood. He died so we could have forgiveness and salvation. He made the ultimate sacrifice on the cross.

S4: We were healed of our sins.

TEACHER: He was a great teacher, teaching us that the only way to heaven is by grace through faith in Him. Jesus was a lifesaver. He saved us from sin, death, and Satan. And on Easter morning He really did come to life! That's what Jesus' saving work is all about—that and so much more.

S2: Didn't I tell you in the first place? It's simple—Jesus saves!

Finish the Lesson

How does the creed serve as a summary of Jesus' work? It lists the various works that Jesus accomplished for our salvation.

What work has Jesus called you and every believer to do? Christ calls us to testify to others about His victory over sin and the grave. He wants all people to know the Good News of salvation.

Closing Prayer

Focus the attention of the group by reciting the Second Article responsively (*LSCE,* p. 14). Then pray this or a similar prayer based on the Second Article:

We praise You, Lord Jesus Christ, that with Your holy, precious blood and Your innocent suffering and death, You purchased and won life for us. Help us to live each day to Your glory. In Your holy name we pray. Amen.

Lesson Suggestions

Hymn: *LW* 353; *TLH* 387; *AGPS* 137

Homework: *LSCE* questions 126–148. Have students write a summary paragraph of what they learned or answer the questions in *Exploring Luther's Small Catechism,* pages 31–36.

Memory Work: Second Article ("who redeemed me … most certainly true")

17

Apostles' Creed, Third Article A

Focus on the Catechism

Focus the attention of the group by reciting the Third Article responsively (*LSCE,* p. 15). Then pray this or a similar prayer based on the Third Article:

We praise You, Holy Spirit, that You have called us to faith by the Gospel. Enlighten and sanctify us this day so that we never fall away from Christ. Strengthen us to forgive one another as Christ forgave us. In His name we pray. Amen.

Activity

Materials: Freshly popped corn

This activity may carry the most impact if it can be done toward the beginning of the lesson. Before class begins, pop several bags of microwave popcorn. Bring the hot bags of popcorn into the room before the students arrive. Let the air in the room fill with the aroma of popcorn. Listen to the students' comments as they enter the room.

Ask students, **Can you identify the smell that is filling the room?** This should not be difficult for the students. **How is the smell making you feel?** Give the students an opportunity to answer. Record responses on the board. **Would you like to taste some of the popcorn that is making the room smell so good?** Again let the students respond to the question. **What makes you think this popcorn is going to taste good?** Let the students respond. The students will more than likely say that the good smell makes them think the popcorn will also taste good.

Say, **Before we taste this popcorn, let's talk about how the smell of the popcorn calls us to eat it. The smell draws our attention to the popcorn. The smell makes us want to eat the freshly popped popcorn. The sense of smell is powerful. It draws us to things that smell good and makes us want to run from things that smell bad.**

God has an even stronger way of drawing us to Himself. God sends the Holy Spirit working through the Gospel of Jesus Christ to draw us to Him. The Third Article of the Apostles' Creed teaches us about the Spirit's work.

Table Talk

(Don't just read—TELL the following true story.)

In 1928 Dr. Alexander Fleming made an unusual discovery. He noticed that stray mold on a bacteria culture prevented the bacteria from growing or spreading. Ten years later, a team of doctors used Fleming's discovery to create penicillin, a drug that stops the spread of bacteria and rescues thousands of patients from death. By receiving penicillin today, patients receive the benefits of medical discoveries made years ago.

The story of penicillin can help us understand how we receive the benefits of Jesus' death and resurrection today. Even though Jesus gave His life for us almost 2,000 years ago, we receive those benefits now when the Holy Spirit applies them to us through Baptism, God's Word, and the Lord's Supper. Through these means, the Holy Spirit gives us the life-saving benefits of Jesus.

Discuss one-on-one or in small groups the following questions. (Mentors will guide students through the lesson sheets.)

➡ Student material starts here.

Jesus is our Savior and we thank Him for His sacrifice on the cross. But how important is the work of the Holy Spirit? Explain your answer.

Essential. If the Holy Spirit did not apply the benefits of Jesus' work to our lives, we would not be saved.

When did the Holy Spirit first give you the benefits of Jesus' death and resurrection?

Students may answer "when I was baptized" or "when I first learned about Jesus in family/church/Sunday school."

What other means of grace does the Holy Spirit use?

The three means of grace are Baptism, the Word, and the Lord's Supper.

Bible Study

After Jesus dies, rises again, and ascends into heaven, the Holy Spirit continues Jesus' ministry through the apostles. Read Acts 2:32–47.

1. Where does Peter state that Jesus is a historical person? That He is the Christ?

In 2:32, 36.

2. Why were these elements necessary in Peter's preaching?

Jesus is a real person who really gave His life for us in order to save us from sin. He fulfills God's promise of a Savior.

3. What effect does Peter's preaching have on the people?

The people were convicted in their hearts and gladly received Baptism.

4. According to the Third Article of the creed, who is behind this effect?

The Holy Spirit has called these people to faith through the Gospel.

5. List as many words or phrases as you can in defining the chief work of the Holy Spirit.

The Holy Spirit guides Peter to preach, causes the people to repent, works in them, washes away their sins in Baptism, and stirs them to devotion.

6. Consider the fact that natural man is "spiritually blind, dead, and an enemy of God," and then review your list. Which of the words or phrases do you think best describes the fact that God, through the power of the Holy Spirit, creates faith in your heart?

Answers will vary.

7. Point out where the Bible story proclaims the Law and the Gospel.

For example, verses 2:38a and 2:40 strongly proclaim the Law. 2:38b–39 proclaims the Gospel.

Family in Faith Journal

Have students recall a time they needed help and their parents helped them. Parents/mentors should record this experience in the Family in Faith Journal.

Fun for Review

Props: Sign reading "LAW," sign reading "GOSPEL," sign reading "Right Path," sign reading "Wrong Path"

Characters: Wrong Crowd (2–3 people), Johnny, Holy Spirit, Narrator

Setting: Arrange the classroom so there are two distinct paths, one showing the "Right Path" and the other the "Wrong Path."

WRONG CROWD (1): *(In front of the Wrong Path sign)* Bummer you got caught drinking, man. Should have used a little mouthwash when you got home. Whadya do? Kiss your mommy goodnight?

(Other dudes laugh and make mock-kissing sounds.)

JOHNNY: No way! Just got busted, that's all. I told my parents I was sorry. They said, "No problem." Sort of.

WRONG CROWD (1): Well, listen! I heard about another party.

WRONG CROWD (2–3): Yeah—let's party! Another chance to ROCK!

WRONG CROWD (1): You with us tonight, Johnny-boy?

JOHNNY: Um, sure.

WRONG CROWD (2): Don't worry. If you do get caught—just give 'em that "I'm sorry" speech again. It worked the first time … *(Exits down Wrong Path)*

JOHNNY: Catch ya later, dudes!

HOLY SPIRIT: *(Spoken out of sight)* Hello, Johnny.

JOHNNY: Hello? Who are you?

HOLY SPIRIT: I am God. God the Holy Spirit, to be precise.

JOHNNY: God? Where are You? I can hear You, but I can't see You.

HOLY SPIRIT: I've been with you since your Baptism into Christ.

JOHNNY: You mean …

HOLY SPIRIT: Yes, I know about the party. It really hurts.

JOHNNY: Like I told my parents, I'm sorry. I know I shouldn't have done that. I know I shouldn't have gone with those guys.

HOLY SPIRIT: Are you truly sorry?

JOHNNY: Sure I am. By the way, God, if You need to help someone else, like later tonight, I'll be okay; go ahead …

HOLY SPIRIT: You're genuinely sorry for going against My will? *And* the will of your parents? Not to mention the will of the state—which says it's illegal for minors to drink?

JOHNNY: I said I was sorry, God! Isn't that enough? *(JOHNNY continues down the Wrong Path.)*

NARRATOR: Johnny continued down the wrong path. But the next day …

JOHNNY: *(Enters praying)* I'm sorry, Lord.

HOLY SPIRIT: *(Holding the Law sign up)* "It is the LORD your God you must follow, and Him you must revere. Keep His commands and obey Him; serve Him and hold fast to Him" (Deuteronomy 13:4).

JOHNNY: I know. I know.

HOLY SPIRIT: "Love the LORD your God with all your heart and with all your soul and with all your strength" (Deuteronomy 6:5).

JOHNNY: I know. I know. I do love You, Lord. But no matter how I try, I fail.

(The Law sign goes down; the Gospel sign goes up.)

HOLY SPIRIT: "But the Lord is faithful, and He will strengthen and protect you from the evil one" (2 Thessalonians 3:3).

JOHNNY: Thank You, Lord. And forgive me.

HOLY SPIRIT: "The LORD is gracious and compassionate, slow to anger and rich in love" (Psalm 145:8).

WRONG CROWD (1): *(Enters)* Johnny-boy! We're back! Let's go!

WRONG CROWD (2–3): Let's ROCK!

(JOHNNY starts to follow them again. And then stops suddenly. The WRONG CROWD keeps walking.)

JOHNNY: *(Talking to himself)* Wait! I said I was sorry! What am I doing?!

(Johnny turns around and goes down the Right Path.)

Finish the Lesson

Who is the Holy Spirit? The Holy Spirit is true God, the third person of the Trinity.

Through what means does the Holy Spirit work? The Holy Spirit works through the Word and the Sacraments, which God has entrusted to the church.

What should it mean when you say you are sorry? "Sorry" shouldn't become an excuse or a tool for getting out of trouble. The Holy Spirit calls us to "repent," to turn from our sins.

Closing Prayer

Focus the attention of the group by reciting the Third Article responsively (*LSCE*, p. 15). Then pray this or a similar prayer based on the Third Article:

We praise You, Holy Spirit, that You have called us to faith by the Gospel. Enlighten and sanctify us this day so that we never fall away from Christ. Strengthen us to forgive one another as Christ forgave us. In His name we pray. Amen.

Lesson Suggestions

Hymn: *LW* 212 or 213; *TLH* 251 or 252; *AGPS* 120

Homework: *LSCE* questions 154–168. Have students write a summary paragraph of what they learned or answer the questions in *Exploring Luther's Small Catechism,* pages 38–40.

Memory Work: Third Article (through "in the true faith"); Psalm 139:7–10 (545); Romans 8:9 (574)

18

Apostles' Creed, Third Article B

Focus on the Catechism

Focus the attention of the group by reciting the Third Article responsively (*LSCE,* p. 15). Then pray this or a similar prayer based on the Third Article:

We praise You, Holy Spirit, that You daily and richly forgive all our sins and the sins of all believers. We pray that You would keep us in the true faith until Christ returns on the Last Day to judge all people. In His name we pray. Amen.

Activity

For this activity you need eight volunteers. Have them face each other in two lines of four people. Ask these volunteers to remove any watches or bracelets. Have each "couple" cross and join hands. These volunteers have formed a human net. Now ask for another volunteer (start with someone light). This volunteer should jump lightly into the arms of the human net. The combined strength of the eight volunteers will support the jumper. Give different people a chance to try the net.

As you end the demonstration, say, **Just as the combined strength of the net helped support each person, God calls us in the church to combine our strengths to support one another. In the church, the Holy Spirit sanctifies and keeps us in the one true faith. He calls us to use His gifts to support one another.**

Table Talk

(Don't just read—TELL the following true story.)

The popular Christian writer Tim LaHaye has created a special series of fictional books called the "Left Behind" series. These popular books have sold more than 7 million copies. One feature of these books that makes them so popular is LaHaye's view of a doctrine called the "rapture." This doctrine states that Jesus will return at the end of time to take all Christians to heaven and leave unbelievers behind to suffer punishment until He returns a second time to judge all people.

LaHaye's twist on this teaching is that people who do not go to heaven in the rapture will have a second chance to repent before the final judgment. LaHaye's teaching is doubly dangerous: the Bible never mentions a rapture and it never teaches that there will be a second chance for repentance after Christ returns.

Discuss one-on-one or in small groups the following questions. (Mentors will guide students through the lesson sheets.)

➡ Student material starts here.

The Bible teaches that Christ will return only once at the end of time. How does the Bible's teaching differ from the rapture teaching?

People who believe in the rapture think Jesus will come back more than once.

Why might someone feel attracted to LaHaye's second-chance doctrine?

Everyone likes another chance, but the Bible teaches that now is the time to repent.

What's dangerous about this teaching?

People who trust LaHaye's teaching may not repent of their sins. Christ may return and find them unbaptized and unprepared for eternal life!

How do false teachings like the rapture undermine and break apart the net of support that God offers through the church?

False teachings tear churches apart and discourage people. Instead of coming to church to be strengthened through God's means of grace, people despise God's Word and God's people.

Bible Study

Because of persecution, the apostle John is exiled to the little island of Patmos. Jesus appears to Him and promises to take care of the church. Read Revelation 1:5b–20.

1. Describe in your own words the picture given in verse 7.

Answers will vary.

2. Since Alpha and Omega are the first and last letters of the Greek alphabet, what is Jesus saying about all of history and the role He plays in it?

Jesus rules all history.

3. What does the apostle John's experience in verse 9 teach you about the place of suffering in a Christian's life?

Christians will experience suffering in this world, but the kingdom of God remains ours. Jesus does not rapture people away from suffering. He supports and strengthens them against suffering and in the midst of suffering.

4. Ask your parent/mentor to share with you why it's comforting through good and bad times to know that Jesus is "the First and the Last … the Living One [who] was dead [but is now] alive forever and ever" (v. 17)?

The Lord rules all history and preserves His people in good times and bad.

5. What are the seven lampstands and where is Jesus in relation to them?

The lampstands represent the churches, and Jesus is in their midst even now.

6. Despite the fact that even within our own church we may have arguments and disagreements, what comfort do we have as Christians?

Jesus is in the midst of our church and strengthens it. He has given us the most powerful cures against trouble: His Word and forgiveness.

7. Can you make the following statement: "If I should die tonight, because of God's grace in Jesus Christ received by my faith in Him, I know for sure I'd go to heaven."

Answers may vary.

8. Point out where the Bible story proclaims the Law and the Gospel.

For example, verse 1:7 proclaims God's judgment on those who reject Christ. 1:5b–6 gently proclaims forgiveness through Christ.

Family in Faith Journal

Students and their parents/mentors should list names of family and friends who are not trusting Christ for salvation and then compose a prayer that the Holy Spirit would lead them to repentance.

Fun for Review

Characters: Announcer, Survivors 1 (male), 2 (male), 3 (female), 4 (female), 5 (male) (Referred to in script as S1–S5)

Setting: Anywhere. Skit begins with S1 and S2 talking to each other; the other SURVIVORS enter when noted.

ANNOUNCER: Welcome to another episode of "Surviving!"—the hit show that follows the lives of people stranded in desperate places. From time to time one member is removed from the group. On our final episode, those surviving will win a precious crown of life. It is up to our group to figure out how they are going to survive. Let's see what the group is up to today.

S1: I don't know about you, but I'm starting to tire of all this.

S2: This is only day 4,732. We've been here 13 years. We could be here another 25,000 days or more, for all we know.

S1: But it seems like the same thing day after day. Same food. Same surroundings. Same people. Same everything. And we never know when we are going to be removed from the group. That's kind of nerve-racking.

S2: It could be worse. There are probably some people trying to figure out how many ways they can cook rats for supper and others eating kangaroo steaks every night. But we have a lot of stress too. Maybe we should form an alliance with some of the others so we'll know who is on our side.

S1: We could stick together and help each other.

S2: But we don't know whom we can trust.

S1: I don't know if I can even trust you! Maybe you're talking to me now because another alliance was formed and you're trying to figure out if I can be trusted!

S2: I'm on your side!

S1: I wonder about Survivor Number 3. She can be very nice, but then something happens and she seems completely different.

S2: I know what you mean. What about Number 5? I can't read him. He seems like a nice guy, but I'm always trying to figure out what's going on in his head.

S1: Number 4 seems like a real brain. She's always thinking, trying to figure things out.

S4: *(Enters)* Hi guys. I was just thinking.

S1: *(to S2)* What did I tell you?

S4: Actually, I was just reading. The book says, "Make every effort to keep the unity of the Spirit through the bond of peace" (Ephesians 4:3). I think the answer to surviving might be right in front of our eyes. I wonder if we are an alliance already, but we end up working against each other? *(Enter S3 and S5.)*

S3: We overheard what you were just saying. I was wondering the same thing. I think that we were chosen for a reason.

S5: What if the head of our group has chosen us to work together and to bring more people into this alliance, and here we are thinking too hard and not trusting each other?

S1: That's an interesting thought. *(To audience)* What do *you* think?

Finish the Lesson

How does this drama illustrate how the church should work? Christ wants us to love and support one another in this world. Though Christians may disagree with one another, they should also lovingly forgive.

What is behind the alliance that Christians form with one another? The Holy Spirit works through God's Word and Sacraments to brings us together as the forgiven people of God.

Closing Prayer

Focus the attention of the group by reciting the Third Article responsively (*LSCE,* p. 15). Then pray this or a similar prayer based on the Third Article:

We praise You, Holy Spirit, that You daily and richly forgive all our sins and the sins of all believers. We pray that You would keep us in the true faith until Christ returns on the Last Day to judge all people. Forgive us when we fail to hold one another up in love. Through Christ we pray. Amen.

Lesson Suggestions

Hymn: *LW* 155; *TLH* 231; *AGPS* 252

Homework: *LSCE* questions 149, 169–179. Have students write a summary paragraph of what they learned or answer the questions in *Exploring Luther's Small Catechism,* pages 40–42.

Memory Work: Third Article ("In the same way … certainly true")

Prayer upon Completing Study of the Apostles' Creed

Following the sermon, the confirmands and their parents/mentors shall come forward. They shall face the congregation, confirmands in front, parents/mentors behind. Then the minister shall say:

Beloved in the Lord, the early Christians summarized the teachings of the Bible in the Apostles' Creed. Across the ages, Christians have used this creed in preparation for Baptism and for public worship.

The students shall then speak together the Apostles' Creed.

Let us pray for our catechumens, that our Lord God would open their hearts and the door of His mercy that they may remain faithful to Christ Jesus, our Lord:

Almighty God and Father, because You always grant growth to Your Church, increase the faith and understanding of our catechumens that, recalling the new birth by the water of Holy Baptism, they may forever continue in the family of those whom You adopt as Your sons and daughters; through Jesus Christ, our Lord.

Response: Amen.

Adapted from *Lutheran Worship*, pp. 205, 276

Morning and Evening Prayers

Focus on the Catechism

Focus the attention of the group by reciting the Morning Prayer responsively (*LSCE*, pp. 30–31). Then pray the following prayer:

Lord, You ask us to pray not just when we feel like it or when we need something, but each day. Prayer is a privilege You give us. Teach us to turn to You each day for forgiveness and help; through Christ, our Lord. Amen.

Activity

Materials: Copies of the Ten Commandments

Have students work in pairs with a copy of the Ten Commandments. As they reflect on each commandment, have them develop a prayer list. The prayers can be either general or specific.

Say, **When we stop and think about it, we have a lot to pray for each day. In his Morning and Evening Prayers, Luther reminds us to commend ourselves to the Lord and daily bring our requests to Him.**

Table Talk

(Don't just read—TELL the following true story.)

A missile ripped through his right wing. His A-4 Fighter whirled about like a 550-mile-an-hour top. Instinctively he reported, "I'm hit," and pulled the ejection handle. As his body launched out of the cockpit, he slammed into the spinning plane, breaking his left leg, right kneecap, and right arm. Only moments after his parachute opened, he crashed into Truc Bach Lake. An angry mob of Vietnamese seized him, dragged him ashore, and beat him.

For five and a half years, pilot John McCain was a prisoner of war. McCain's years of beating, ridicule, and solitary confinement nearly destroyed him. But in the midst of this terror he continued to pray and even testified to his faith in Christ before his captors. Once, after an especially cruel interrogation, McCain was thrown into a new cell. Alone in the darkness, hopelessly cut off from all other believers, and feeling abandoned by God, he noted some scratches on the cell wall. Looking closer he recognized these faded words, "I believe in God, the Father Almighty"—the opening words of the Apostles' Creed. He recalled the unending promise of God's presence and love. At that moment, a fellow prisoner's confession and prayer rescued McCain's heart from despair.

Discuss one-on-one or in small groups the following questions. (Mentors will guide students through the lesson sheets.)

➡ Student material starts here.

What role did daily prayer play in McCain's imprisonment?

Prayer was a great gift God gave to McCain in the face of bitter suffering.

How did the discovery that other prisoners were praying affect McCain?

It inspired and encouraged him.

Why might McCain continue to pray after he was set free?

When you see the comfort, hope, and assurance God provides through His Gospel in answer to prayer, how could you ever stop?

Bible Study

Some of God's people being held in captivity in Babylon sought to stay there because they were enmeshed in the materialism of Babylon. Those who left were spiritually motivated to rebuild the temple and to reestablish Jerusalem. Read Ezra 3:1–6.

1. **When did they make sacrifices?**

Morning and evening.

2. **What were God's people willing to do despite the fear of the people who surrounded them? See 3:3–6.**

They continued to work together to rebuild the temple, their place of prayer.

3. **When we do God's work, who ridicules or frightens us?**

Answers may vary.

4. **In the Old Testament, God's people worshipped at the temple. What has taken the place of the temple and its sacrifices?**

The church and the daily prayers we offer through Christ.

5. **Prayer is not a "means of grace"—a way in which the Holy Spirit offers us the blessings of Christ and creates faith in us. If prayer does not give us God's grace, why then do we pray?**

God tenderly invites us to pray and promises to hear us and act on our behalf. We pray because God is gracious.

6. **How do the blessings we receive during the worship service and family devotions help us with the fears we face?**

Through His Word and Sacraments and the mutual consolation of the brethren (Smalcald Articles IV), God emboldens us to serve Him and encourage one another.

7. **Why make the sign of the holy cross before praying the Morning or Evening Prayers?**

The sign of the cross reminds us that we were baptized into Christ in the name of the Father and of the Son and of the Holy Spirit. God has marked us with the cross as His own people.

8. **As you examine Luther's daily prayers, which words or statements are most meaningful to you?**

Answers will vary.

9. **Point out where the Bible story proclaims the Law and the Gospel.**

For example, verse 3:2 proclaims the Law. The whole passage focuses on following the old covenant laws about worship. The entire Old Testament ceremonial Law pointed to Christ and His atoning sacrifice for the sins of the world.

Family in Faith Journal

Parents or mentors should share how prayer has helped them face life courageously and confidently. They should record the story in the Family in Faith Journal.

Fun for Review

Characters: 1, 2, and 3

Setting: Performed in readers' theater style.

1: Pray without ceasing.

2: Pray without sleeping?

1: No. Pray without *ceasing.*

3: *Play* without ceasing?

1: No. *Pray* without *ceasing.*

2: No stopping?

3: Impossible.

1: All things are possible with God.

2: Can I pray while I sleep?

3: Can I pray while I play?

1: Commend yourself to God's care.

2: I commend my sleep to God's care.

3: I commend my play to God's care.

1: Commend your morning. Commend your evening.

2: Give your all to God.

3: Morning and evening.

1: Sleeping and waking.

2: Sleep in peace, trusting in God.

3: Sleep in peace, being a good manager of your bodies.

1: Play with joy.

2: Work with joy.

3: Who's Joy?

1: Joy comes with peace.

2: Peace and joy come in commending your all to God.

1: Morning and evening.

3: Waking and sleeping.

2: Pray continually.

1: That's what I say.

3: That's what God says.

2: That's what Paul says.

3: 1 Thessalonians 5:17.

1: Pray with thanksgiving.

2: Pray for forgiveness.

3: Pray for protection.

1: Pray to the Father through Jesus Christ.

2: Play in His name.

3: Thankfully play.

1: Play, protected by angels.

2: Live forgiven.

3: Pray without ceasing.

1: In the name of the Father.

2: In the name of the Son.

3. In the name of the Holy Spirit.

1: Amen.

2: Amen.

3: So be it!

Finish the Lesson

How often do you pray? Answers will vary.

How is it possible to pray without ceasing? Because our sinful minds are easily distracted, we fail to pray as we should. However, we can pray at any time or anywhere. We can pray aloud or in our hearts.

Closing Prayer

Focus the attention of the group by reciting the Evening Prayer responsively. Then pray the following prayer based on these prayers:

Lord, You ask us to pray not just when we feel like it or when we need something, but each day. Prayer is a privilege You give us. Teach us to turn to You each day for forgiveness and help; through Christ, our God. Amen.

Lesson Suggestions

Hymn: *LW* 424; *TLH* 535; *AGPS* 261

Homework: *LSCE* questions 193–204. Have students write a summary paragraph of what they learned or answer the questions in *Exploring Luther's Small Catechism,* pages 44–45.

Memory Work: Morning and Evening Prayers; 1 Thessalonians 5:16–18 (685); Psalm 50:15 (717)

Lord's Prayer, Introduction and Conclusion

Focus on the Catechism

Focus the attention of the group by reciting the Introduction and Conclusion of the Lord's Prayer responsively (*LSCE,* pp. 17, 20). Then pray this or a similar prayer based on the Introduction and Conclusion of the Lord's Prayer:

Dear Father in heaven, thanks for making us Your true children through Your Son, Jesus Christ. Give us all boldness and confidence to seek Your help each day and to live as Your dear children; through Christ, our Lord. Amen.

Activity

Materials: Cell phone and pager

Show the cell phone and pager to the class. Ask, **Can you explain how these two communication devices work? How is it that I can punch numbers into this device** (go ahead and send a page) **and know that in a few minutes a message will be sent to this pager?** Let the students share their answers. Emphasize that we cannot see the electrical signals being sent from one device to the other. However, we trust that when we use them, they will work. When the pager finally sounds, remind the class that it is amazing that someone across town or across the state can get my attention by simply punching a few numbers into a phone.

Say, **However, what is even more amazing is knowing that we have a way of getting God's attention whenever we need Him: prayer. The next several lessons will help you understand just how important prayer is to God and you. God our Father wants us to be bold and confident when we pray to Him. In fact, God invites us and even commands us to pray to Him, and He promises to hear us for Jesus' sake. Our heavenly Father wants us to keep in touch.**

Table Talk

(Don't just read—TELL the following true story.)

When missionary Amy Hartwig married Marat Kashenov in Kazakhstan (part of the old Soviet Union), their wedding ceremony sparked exciting conversation among Marat's family members. Most of Marat's family were not Christian. But while they ate together, Marat's father jokingly suggested that by next year they might all become Lutheran Christians.

As the guests chuckled, an uncle asked why everyone was laughing. He pointed out that because of this wedding service, all of them were now thinking and talking about God—something they had not done in a very long time. Although Marat's father was joking, God's Word was at work, changing their hearts.

Discuss one-on-one or in small groups the following questions. (Mentors will guide students through the lesson sheets.)

➡ Student material starts here.

How did the words and prayers offered during the wedding service affect Marat's family?

Through the Word of God, the Holy Spirit was calling Marat's family to faith. God was answering the prayers of blessing even as the pastor spoke them!

Do we grow in faith because we pray, or do we pray because we grow in faith?

We pray because we grow in faith. Faith comes through God's Word and encourages us to pray.

What challenges might Marat and Amy experience because Marat's family are not yet Christians? What opportunities might they have?

The family may not always understand Marat and Amy's commitment to the Lord. Marat and Amy will have many opportunities to tell the family about Jesus.

Bible Study

When sinners gather to hear Jesus teach, the Pharisees feel offended. Then Jesus tells a parable. Read Luke 15:11–24.

1. What was Jesus' main point of telling the story of the prodigal son?

God is a gracious and forgiving Father.

2. Describe a time when you resembled each of these characters in one way or another: (a) the Prodigal Son, (b) the father.

Answers will vary.

3. Read verse 21. Does the son really have faith in his father's forgiveness?

No. The son can't believe that his father will accept him as a son again. This is the speech he rehearsed in verse 19.

4. Read aloud verse 20. Does the prodigal son say anything to his father before the father embraces him? What assurance do you receive from that thought?

No. We don't have to convince God to love us. He eagerly desires to forgive us.

5. How did the son come to believe the father would forgive him? See Luke 15:22.

The words of the father change his heart. God's Word works the same way. By our own reason or strength, we cannot believe in Him. But His Word changes us and grants us faith.

6. What boldness does this story give us when it comes to approaching God in prayer, even when we've been disobedient and far away from Him?

Our heavenly Father loves us and will forgive us through Christ.

7. As we spend time in prayer, praying according to God's Word, how might God change us?

Answers will vary. Remind the students that praying helps us focus more on God's goodness and what He wants for us. God wants to be a greater part of our lives.

8. Point out where the story proclaims the Law and the Gospel.

For example, 15:17–19 shows how the son's guilt condemned him. Luke 15:20b points to the father's forgiveness.

Family in Faith Journal

Have students list five words that describe a father and discuss them with their parents/mentors. How do they apply to the heavenly Father? Record the discussion in the Family in Faith Journal.

Fun for Review

Props: Play food and cooking utensils, apron (a chef's hat would be nice), trays and napkins—items a waiter may use

Characters: Pierre, the Head Chef (give it your best French accent!); Lost Son; Servants (2–3); Forgiving Father

Setting: The back kitchen

(SERVANTS are gathered around PIERRE. He speaks with nervous excitement.)

PIERRE: You should have seen it! Day after day, Monsieur was waiting at the end of the driveway. It was truly a sad sight to behold. Ah, the poor old man. He would scan the horizon, until one afternoon, voila! He sees his son coming in the distance! *(Clapping hands for orders)* And now, here we are. We are to throw a party! And a party it will be!

FORGIVING FATHER: *(Rushes in)* Okay! Okay! Pierre? Make everything right! I want the best fattened calf we've got. I want it to be a great feast! For this son of mine was dead and is alive again; he was lost and is found! LET'S CELEBRATE! *(Exits)*

PIERRE: We have work to do! You! Get the best, largest calf we have! And you! Come here and grate this parmesan cheese! Snap to it, rapidement! Now we need someone to help set the table … you! Come here!

LOST SON: *(Turns and points to himself)* Me, sir?

PIERRE: Ahhhhh! What are you doing here? Does your father know you're here? You don't belong here! This place is for the servants. You're not a servant. You're a son! You are an heir of this house!

LOST SON: But I don't deserve to be a son. I don't even deserve to be at the table. Pierre, let me work back here with you! I will be a good servant. I promise!

PIERRE: Ahhhhh! No! No, you can't! Did you not hear what your pa-pa has told you? You were lost! And now? You are found!

LOST SON: Yes, but I don't deserve what my father has said. Let me work here for a while—a few weeks, maybe. Then I can say I actually earned my way back.

PIERRE: Ahhhhh, contraire! No! I will not have it! This is not something for you to earn. It is by the grace of your father that he has welcomed you back to the house!

FORGIVING FATHER: My son! My son! What are you doing in here? You should be out there with the guests. You are not a slave; you are my dear son.

SERVANTS (1–3): Slaves?

PIERRE: Quiet, you! I'll explain later. Back to work!

LOST SON: I've embarrassed you, Dad. I've embarrassed the family name. Now I deserve nothing but the crumbs that fall from the kitchen counter.

FORGIVING FATHER: Yes, you are right.

LOST SON: I am?

PIERRE: Ahhhhh! No worry! We will prepare the best parmesan crumbs in the world!

FORGIVING FATHER: Pierre, please. Just make the feast. *(PIERRE goes to work with SERVANTS.)* Son, you do not deserve even the title of slave. But I forgive you. And by this forgiveness you are made whole again and are once again an heir to this estate. Now come, let us go to the banquet table.

(FORGIVING FATHER and LOST SON embrace, then exit.)

Finish the Lesson

Why was the son hiding out in the kitchen among the servants? He knew he didn't deserve to be his father's son anymore.

Do you have times when you doubt God's forgiveness? What should you do? Most Christians experience times of doubt. However, through His Word the Lord stirs our hearts to faith.

Closing Prayer

Focus the attention of the group by reciting the Introduction and Conclusion of the Lord's Prayer responsively (*LSCE,* pp. 17, 20). Then pray this or a similar prayer based on the Introduction and Conclusion of the Lord's Prayer:

Dear Father who art in heaven, thanks for making us Your true children through Your Son, Jesus Christ. Give us all boldness and confidence to seek Your help each day and live as Your dear children; through Christ, our Lord. Amen.

Lesson Suggestions

Hymn: *LW* 431:1, 9; *TLH* 458; *AGPS* 95

Homework: *LSCE* questions 205-207, 234-235. Have students write a summary paragraph of what they learned or answer the questions in *Exploring Luther's Small Catechism,* page 46.

Memory Work: Introduction and Conclusion to the Lord's Prayer; 2 Corinthians 6:18 (720); James 1:17 (823)

Lord's Prayer, First and Second Petitions

Focus on the Catechism

Focus the attention of the group by reciting the First and Second Petitions of the Lord's Prayer responsively (*LSCE,* pp. 17–18). Then pray this or a similar prayer based on the First and Second Petitions:

Dear Father who art in heaven, You have made us holy members of Your kingdom through Jesus. As Your dear children, help us to lead holy lives each day and share the promise of Your kingdom with others; through Christ, our Lord. Amen.

Activity

Materials: Sign with "WALK" printed on it, sign with "STOP" printed on it

Have students stand at the far end of the room, opposite from where you are standing. Don't give them further instructions. Hold up the sign that says "WALK"; after a few seconds hold up the sign that says "STOP." Repeat this until the students are standing in front of you.

Say, **You moved across the room without me saying anything. How did you know what I wanted you to do?** Let the class respond. The students will point out that they had written instructions. Say, **These written words communicated ideas to you. The words changed your actions. The words instructed you when to walk and when to stop. Somewhat similarly, God changes us through His Word. Through His Word the Spirit brings us to faith in Jesus, our Savior. Through His Word the Spirit empowers us to stop misusing God's name and to walk in God's ways, to hallow God's name. In the First and Second Petitions of the Lord's Prayer we ask God to change our lives by His Word.**

Table Talk

(Don't just read—TELL the following true story.)

When a young woman from China came to study at East Lansing, Michigan, Marcia Mittwede told her about Jesus, her Savior, and encouraged her to read the Bible. But as the young woman began to read, she received bad news from home: her mother was sick. She would have to go back to China. When the young woman left, Marcia Mittwede wondered whether she would continue to read the Bible or forget about it when she got home.

Then Marcia received a message from the young woman. In the note she explained that her time of study in the United States had not only introduced her to academic subjects but had also introduced her to God. After she returned home, she visited a Christian church there and greatly enjoyed the service. She promised to continue reading the Bible and learning about God.

Discuss one-on-one or in small groups the following questions. (Mentors will guide students through the lesson sheets.)

➡ Student material starts here.

How did God's kingdom touch the life of this young woman?

Marcia Mittwede shared the Gospel with her and introduced her to the Bible.

Can a Christian hallow God's name and serve God's kingdom alone, or does each Christian need a congregation?

Though we can hallow God's name individually, God calls us to hallow His name together. Remember, we are His kingdom and pray to "our Father."

How does your congregation help you to hallow God's name and live in His kingdom?

Through God's Word and Sacraments.

Bible Study

Nicodemus, a great religious and political leader, sneaks in to visit Jesus at night. Jesus tells him about the kingdom of God. Read John 3:1–8.

1. The Greek phrase "born again" can mean being "born from above." In what way is our rebirth truly something that takes place from "above" (see also 1 Corinthians 2:14)?

No one can give birth to himself. God must give us the new birth through faith in Christ Jesus.

2. What response did Nicodemus have when Jesus said one must be born again to enter the kingdom of God?

He did not understand what Jesus meant. He thought of natural birth instead of spiritual rebirth.

3. What does Jesus describe when He refers to "water and the Spirit"?

He is referring to Baptism, which gets its power from the Word connected with the water.

4. Through water and the Holy Spirit, God makes us holy. Name specific ways you keep God's name holy.

Answers will vary.

5. Are there some family members or friends at school who have not entered the "kingdom of God"? If so, include these people in your prayers, asking that God would use you and others to bring God's kingdom to them.

6. Point out where the Bible story proclaims the Law and the Gospel.

For example, 3:6 states that the flesh only gives birth to flesh. In contrast, it also states that the Spirit of God gives us the new spiritual birth of Baptism.

Family in Faith Journal

Parents/mentors should complete the following statement: "All children are special. But I especially thank God for my child because … ." Have students write the response in the Family in Faith Journal.

Fun for Review

Props: 2 chairs

Characters: Rick, a TV show host; Nic(odemus)

Setting: Television-program set. RICK and NIC are sitting.

RICK: Hello! I'm Rick, your host tonight. We have a special guest on the show. Please welcome Nic at Night to our "Nic at Night" show! Whoa, that's cool. You have the same name as our show. That's so cool! Well, Nic, why don't you start by telling us about yourself?

NIC: Thank you for having me. Nic is short for Nicodemus. I used to be a Pharisee, a member of the Jewish ruling council in Jerusalem.

RICK: Fascinating, Nic, simply fascinating.

NIC: I received the rest of my nickname because I went to talk to Jesus one night. I wasn't brave enough to be seen with Him during the day. That's why people call me Nic at Night—get it?

RICK: I think so, Nic.

NIC: But all that has changed for me now. I guess I should be called "Nic in the Light"!

RICK: How were you changed?

NIC: It's a matter of who and what changed me, first of all.

RICK: Who? What? When? Where? Take a stab at them all, Nic!

NIC: The "who" is Jesus Christ. He's the one I went to talk to and He's the one who changed me. He told me that no one can see the kingdom of God unless he is born again.

RICK: I bet that about floored you, Nic.

NIC: Just about, Rick. I didn't understand everything He was telling me at the time, but now I fully understand because He changed me through His Word and through Baptism.

RICK: Words can change people, Nic at Night who's now in the light, right?

NIC: I am walking in the light of Jesus Christ. His Word changed my life, Rick. The Holy Spirit changes people. He brings them forgiveness. He places His holy name on them. He gives them eternal life. He brings them out of the darkness of sin into His perfect light.

RICK: So the sin is like darkness. And His Holy Spirit uses God's Word and Baptism to bring people into His light? Is that right, Nic?

NIC: That's right, Rick.

RICK: Wow.

NIC: Wow, indeed! And now instead of being in the kingdom of the Pharisees I am part of the kingdom of God! I live in His light.

RICK: So you're not scared to talk about Jesus Christ in public anymore?

NIC: No more wimping out and meeting Jesus in the dark. We walk together in His light. I am not ashamed of Jesus or His holy name or His perfect light and life.

RICK: You are really pumped about this Jesus, aren't you, Nic?

NIC: I am, Rick. His kingdom has come to me. His name is holy to me. And I have been changed by the Holy Spirit's power, working through God's Word.

RICK: It sounds like no more "Nic at Night" for you, huh?

NIC: Forget sneaking around at night. I want to forget everyone the light of Jesus. I'm Nic in the Light! Nic in the Light! Nic in the Light!

Finish the Lesson

What changed Nic at Night? The Holy Spirit changed him through the Word so that he was born again in Christ.

Where do we find confidence to talk about Jesus publicly? The Holy Spirit also encourages us to witness to others.

Closing Prayer

Focus the attention of the group by reciting the First and Second Petitions of the Lord's Prayer responsively (*LSCE,* pp. 17–18). Then pray this or a similar prayer based on the First and Second Petitions:

Dear Father who art in heaven, You have made us holy members of Your kingdom through Jesus. As Your dear children, help us to lead holy lives each day and share the promise of Your kingdom with others. Overcome our fears through Christ, our Lord. Amen.

Lesson Suggestions

Hymn: *LW* 431:1–3; *TLH* 458; *AGPS* 115

Homework: *LSCE* questions 208–214. Have students write a summary paragraph of what they learned or answer the questions in *Exploring Luther's Small Catechism,* pages 47–48.

Memory work: First and Second Petitions; Psalm 54:1; Colossians 1:13–14 (742)

Lord's Prayer, Third Petition

Focus on the Catechism

Focus the attention of the group by reciting the Third Petition of the Lord's Prayer responsively (*LSCE,* p. 18). Then pray this or a similar prayer based on the Third Petition:

Our Father who art in heaven, You break and hinder every evil plan and purpose of the devil so that we may hallow Your name and live in Your kingdom. Strengthen and keep us firm in Your Word and faith this day and every day until we die; through Christ, our Lord. Amen.

Activity

Materials: Overhead or slide projector, transparency or picture of tablets of the Ten Commandments

Begin by saying that you have a picture to show the class. Turn on the projector, but make certain that it is very out of focus. Ask the class to identify the picture. (They should have difficulty doing so.) Let the students offer a few suggestions. Say, **God's Word teaches us about God's will for us and for all the world. However, the devil, the world, and our sinful nature work against God's Word. They try to keep it out of focus. The devil, the world, and our sinful nature try to distort God's Word so that we cannot see or understand God's will. How do you think God's Word might be distorted?** Write the students' responses on the board.

Ask, **What might make this picture clearer?** The class will suggest that you focus the projector. As you begin doing this, say, **In the Third Petition of the Lord's Prayer we ask for God's help to do His will. We ask Him to break the ways that make His Word and will unclear and to strengthen us in His Word and will, so that we grow strong in our faith in Jesus. What does God do to make His Word and His will clearer in our lives?** Record the students' suggestions. (God provides people to help us understand His Word. He also gives us the ability to pray and to ask for understanding.)

Table Talk

(Don't just read—TELL the following true story.)

In 1915 Rosa Young and other African-American teachers like her faced a terrible dilemma. Shortly after Rosa started the Rosebud school for the children of Alabama sharecroppers, the Mexican boll weevil invaded the fields and ruined the farmers' crops. The families lost their ability to support the school. Rosa had to dismiss two teachers. And at the end of the school year, she had only $12.85 left to pay teachers' salaries.

But Rosa refused to give up. She began contacting different organizations and leaders, hoping to find someone who would support the school. Then Rosa received a letter from the famous educator Dr. Booker T. Washington. He encouraged her to write to the Lutheran church for help because they were doing so much for African-American children in other parts of the country. Rosa wrote a letter offering to give the school property to the Lutherans if they would help keep it going.

After meeting Rosa and visiting the school, the Lutherans said "yes!" The school was rescued and a new church started. The next spring, 58 people were baptized and 70 were confirmed—including Rosa! Through her, God had turned a terrible situation into an incredible blessing.

Discuss one-on-one or in small groups the following questions. (Mentors will guide students through the lesson sheets.)

➡ Student material starts here.

What might Rosa's neighbors have said about God's will when Rosa had only $12.85 left to run her school?

Some may have told her that it was not God's will that they have a school.

Before Rosa had prayed and sought help for the school, could she have guessed what God's will was? Explain your answer.

Not really. We can't tell God's will from circumstances. However, God's Word may have encouraged Rosa to keep going against all odds.

If circumstances can't tell us God's will, where can we learn God's will?

The Bible reveals God's will for our lives, not by answering specific questions like "Should I start a school?" but by telling us how God serves us through Christ and how we should live.

What is the most important thing God wants for each of us?

He wants us to come to faith in Jesus and be saved.

Bible Study

Joseph's brothers scheme to get rid of him. When a caravan of merchantmen comes along, they sell Joseph and tell their father that Joseph has been brutally killed by an animal. Years later, they discover he is still alive when they come to Egypt for food because of a famine. Read Genesis 45:1-7.

1. Despite the brother's plans, God had a different plan. What was God's plan according to Joseph? See verses 5–7.

To preserve the people's lives by storing up food.

2. Have you ever argued over God's will? What was it over? Who won the argument?

Answers will vary.

3. How do you think Joseph's brothers felt after discovering that God's will was far different from theirs?

Surprised but pleased.

4. Name some of the things that we know are God's will.

Answers will vary. Examples should be the commandments, the saving love of God in Christ, prayer, and so on.

5. Identify times when you've found it difficult to do God's will. What forces hindered you from doing it?

Answers will vary.

6. What does the forgiveness that Joseph offers to his brothers teach us about God's will?

God wants us to forgive one another.

7. How vital is forgiveness to the life of a Christian?

Forgiveness through Christ (justification) is the central teaching of the Christian faith.

8. Point out where the story proclaims the Law and the Gospel.

For example, 45:3 refers to the fear the sinner experiences, while 45:5–7 gently proclaims God's mercy.

Family in Faith Journal

Parents/mentors should describe to the students a time when they were not sure what God's will was for their lives. The students should ask how things were resolved and record the story.

Fun for Review

Prop: Kleenex

Characters: Joseph, Rueben, Benjamin, Zebulun, Simeon, Levi, Judah, Issachar

Setting: Genesis 45:15—at the palace. Everyone is blowing his nose, tearful yet happy.

JOSEPH: Brothers! Brothers! Listen. It is good to be here with you. After Dan, Naphtali, Gad, and Asher return with our father, we will have a great celebration! In the meantime, let's talk about what happened. Isn't this so cool?

RUEBEN: What's cool?

JOSEPH: How I got here!

BENJAMIN: *(Still sobbing)* You mean you're not mad at us?

ALL BROTHERS: BENJAMIN!

JOSEPH: No. I am not. In fact, I am amazed at the way our God works. When you guys sold me into slavery, I was scared. Then it became apparent that God was at work here. If you hadn't been jealous of me, this would have never happened! Isn't that great?

RUEBEN: No. I mean, we're glad you're okay, Joseph. But we never should have faked your death. We never should have been jealous of Dad's love for you.

ZEBULUN: *(Looking at BENJAMIN)* Benny, is that really Joseph?

BENJAMIN: *(Starting to cry louder)* Yes. Yes, it is!

ZEBULUN: Wow!

JOSEPH: I know you shouldn't have, Rueben. But isn't it amazing how God can use our sinful acts to bring about blessings? It was God's will. This was God's will! By the way, what did you do with my coat?

SIMEON: Coat?

LEVI: Um, well, you see …

JUDAH: It was God's will that we tear it …

ISSACHAR: And it was God's will that we put animal blood on it …

RUEBEN: And then, well, it was His will that we throw it away.

SIMEON: It looked pretty yucky.

BENJAMIN: Ohhh, the coat!

ZEBULUN: Joseph? You okay?

JOSEPH: You threw it away! I wouldn't call what you did with my coat "God's will." That's stretching it a bit, bros. Oh well, it doesn't really matter. That coat is a distant memory. What's important now is that there's a deliverance!

RUEBEN: You're right! Dad will be so glad!

SIMEON: I'm actually looking forward to Goshen.

ISSACHAR: It's time to leave the ranch!

LEVI: Yee haw!

Finish the Lesson

How did God accomplish His will in Joseph's life? He rescued Joseph from imprisonment. God worked through the bad things in Joseph's life to accomplish good.

How does the example of Joseph help you understand the struggles you may face in life? When I face difficult times, I can trust that God will be at work through them. He will work for my good and the good of those around me.

Closing Prayer

Focus the attention of the group by reciting the Third Petition of the Lord's Prayer responsively (*LSCE,* p. 18). Then pray this or a similar prayer based on the Third Petition:

Our Father who art in heaven, You break and hinder every evil plan and purpose of the devil so that we may hallow Your name and live in Your kingdom. Strengthen and keep us firm in Your Word and faith this day and every day until we die. Forgive us when we doubt Your will; through Christ, our Lord. Amen.

Lesson Suggestions

Hymn: *LW* 431:1, 3; *TLH* 458

Homework: *LSCE* questions 215–218. Have students write a summary paragraph of what they learned or answer the questions in *Exploring Luther's Small Catechism,* page 49.

Memory Work: Third Petition; John 6:40 (751); Romans 7:18 (756)

Lord's Prayer, Fourth Petition

Focus on the Catechism

Focus the attention of the group by reciting the Fourth Petition of the Lord's Prayer responsively (*LSCE,* pp. 18–19). Then pray this or a similar prayer based on the Fourth Petition:

Our Father who art in heaven, You give us everything we need each day. Help us not only to give thanks for Your generosity but also to share the abundance of Your blessings; through Christ, our Lord. Amen.

Activity

Materials: Lamp, 2 light bulbs (one working and one burned out)

Plug in the lamp and ask the students where the power to light the bulb comes from. Then turn on the lamp. However, make certain that you have put the burned-out bulb in the lamp so there is no light. Ask, **Why isn't the light coming on?** Students may offer a variety of answers.

Replace the burned-out bulb with a working bulb and then turn the lamp on. Ask, **What is the difference?** The students will understand that the difference is in the bulbs. One works and one does not work. Help them understand that the power source is the same. The lamp is the same, but the bulbs are different. That is the point of this petition. Say, **God supplies all people with daily bread: what they need to survive, the power of life. Some people will never acknowledge His good gifts. Like the burned-out bulb, they receive the power, but they are unwilling or unable to acknowledge it. Others realize that God is the provider. They realize that God gives us everything we need, including the forgiveness and salvation Jesus earned at Calvary. And they are thankful. As the Fourth Petition teaches, their grateful attitude shines forth.**

Table Talk

(Don't just read—TELL the following true story.)

In October 1929 the booming U.S. economy suddenly crashed, helping to cause the Great Depression across the country. A few years later, one out of every three workers had lost his job. To make matters worse, it stopped raining in many parts of the country. Violent winds swept across the dry fields, tossing huge, black clouds of farm ground into the air. Dust piled up like snowdrifts. Nothing would grow. People fled from their homes in search of work. For many, it seemed like the end of the world.

But Miriam Long of Selma, Alabama, remembers things differently. She remembers that her aunts and uncles, while searching for work, would often come to visit and stay at her house. When her father walked around the city looking for electrical repair jobs, Miriam followed and remembers meeting hundreds of new and interesting people. She remembers the family garden and "Dotsy" the milk cow that they kept in the backyard. She remembers how the quest for food brought families and neighbors together. For Miriam, the Great Depression and the droughts of the 1930s were years of wonder. As she prayed each day for daily bread, she never doubted that God heard her and took care of her.

Discuss one-on-one or in small groups the following questions. (Mentors will guide students through the lesson sheets.)

➡ Student material starts here.

Does hardship mean that God has abandoned us? Explain your answer.

No. God preserves His people in the face of hardship.

What in Miriam's experience gave her confidence in God's care?

Despite their poverty, her family had enough to keep them going. She learned to appreciate the more important gifts that God gives, like family.

Why pray for daily bread if you have enough to eat?

To offer thanks and acknowledge that God is the giver of all good gifts.

Bible Study

Paul is confronted in Athens with a city full of idols and people who philosophize about life and death. Paul presents the people with new hope through the preaching of the Gospel. Read Acts 17:16–31.

1. How does verse 21 describe many people today in their search for spirituality?

People often focus on the latest thing instead of focusing on what is true, lasting, and faithful.

2. How does Paul describe God as a personal Creator and Designer of all things?

Answers should reflect Paul's description in 17:24–29.

3. What comfort do you receive from knowing that God has not left things to happen by chance?

He guides every part of our life. We are not ruled by fate but a loving Father.

4. According to Paul, where do all good things come from?

God alone.

5. If God owns everything, including the power of life and death, what would God have you do with your life?

Faithfully devote it to His service.

6. If God gives us daily bread without our asking, why do some people worry about not having enough?

Worry comes from a lack of trust in God's promise. However, others may take God's promise as an excuse to not work.

7. Can you identify someone who does not have the "daily bread" he/she needs to survive? Name some things you and your mentor might do to help this person.

Answers may vary. People in other nations are often hungry because of corrupt government and war. Sin causes such starvation, not a lack of God's bounty.

8. Point out where the Bible story proclaims the Law and the Gospel.

For example, 17:29–30 strongly proclaims the Law. The crowd interrupts Paul as he begins to preach the Gospel of the resurrection of Jesus.

9. What does Christ provide for you that is even more precious than daily bread?

Forgiveness, life, and salvation.

Family in Faith Journal

Have students describe a memorable Thanksgiving Day meal. The parents/mentors should record this memory in the Family in Faith Journal.

Fun for Review

Characters: Marco, Katerina

KATERINA: Hi, Marco! What did you think about that special presentation on future vocations?

MARCO: I was disappointed at first because I thought it was about future **vacations**!

KATERINA: *(Laughing)* I guess you were surprised to find us discussing future jobs instead of travel plans to the mountains or beach! But did you find the presentation helpful?

MARCO: It made me think. I've thought about a lot of different jobs I might work at someday.

KATERINA: Like what?

MARCO: A couple of years ago I wanted to be an airplane pilot. Then I realized pilots don't have much employment security since their jobs are always up in the air.

KATERINA: Very funny! That's kind of a *plane* job anyway!

MARCO: Then I thought about being a baseball player, but that might drive me *batty*.

KATERINA: I figured you would have *a ball* in that profession.

MARCO: How about you, Katerina? You enjoy basketball.

KATERINA: I figure at my height I won't have *a shot* at being a professional woman's basketball player.

MARCO: I agree. But after today's seminar, I'm thinking about being a bread delivery person.

KATERINA: What made you think about that job?

MARCO: Think about it. There's a lot of *loafing* around! I wouldn't loaf around, of course, because I'd want to do a good job for my employer, who will be paying me a lot of *dough* for my work!

KATERINA: Those are, ummm, interesting thoughts!

MARCO: It also seems like it has more job security than any other job.

KATERINA: Why do you say that?

MARCO: Everyone wants bread. Everyone wants bread every day. There must be a great need for bread delivery people.

KATERINA: I guess people eat a lot of bread.

MARCO: Just think about it. Don't you think that all over the world "The Lord's Prayer" must be prayed a million times a day?

KATERINA: I guess. But now you're confusing me.

MARCO: Every time "The Lord's Prayer" is prayed by someone, they pray, "Give us this day our daily bread." People want bread so much that they're praying for it. The world needs people to deliver that bread. And that will be me.

KATERINA: *(Laughing)* I have a funny feeling you're not joking this time.

MARCO: It's nothing to joke about.

KATERINA: No, it isn't. But I need to explain something to you. When people are praying, "Give us this day our daily bread," they aren't asking for wheat, white, or rye.

MARCO: Really?

KATERINA: Really! The phrase "daily bread" means anything that supports our daily life.

MARCO: Well, if that is true, I guess the job of delivering "daily bread" is already taken.

KATERINA: What do you mean?

MARCO: The only true "daily bread deliverer" is God. He's the one who gives us all that we need.

KATERINA: He certainly does deliver! But God also uses His people to bring others what they need. So whatever job you end up having, there will be part of a "daily bread delivery person" in you!

MARCO: I like that thought, Kat! Since that is the case, maybe I'll just do what my dad does for a living. He repairs shoes. He's always said that he's in the business of saving *soles*!

Finish the Lesson

How does God deliver bread to you and all people? Through the fruit of the earth, the labor of my neighbors, and my own work.

Name some daily bread God has delivered to you today. Answers will vary.

Closing Prayer

Focus the attention of the group by reciting the Fourth Petition of the Lord's Prayer responsively (*LSCE*, pp. 18–19). Then pray this or a similar prayer based on the Fourth Petition:

Our Father who art in heaven, You give us everything we need each day. Help us not only to give thanks for Your generosity but also to share the abundance of Your blessings; through Christ, our Lord. Amen.

Lesson Suggestions

Hymn: *LW* 431:1, 5; *TLH* 458; *AGPS* 207

Homework: *LSCE* questions 219–222. Have students write a summary paragraph of what they learned or answer the questions in *Exploring Luther's Small Catechism*, pages 49–50.

Memory Work: Fourth Petition; Matthew 6:33 (774); 1 Timothy 6:8 (784)

24

Blessing and Thanksgiving

Focus on the Catechism

Focus the attention of the group by reciting the Table Prayers responsively (*LSCE*, pp. 31–32).

Activity

Materials: Sheet of paper with the words "Blessings and Thanksgiving" written in very small print, binoculars, tape, board, markers

Tape the paper in a corner of the room where it will be difficult to read the words. Select a volunteer to read the writing on the paper you hung in the corner of the room. Remember, it should be impossible to read the writing with only the naked eye. After the volunteer has tried to read the writing, ask the class for suggestions on what might make reading the words easier. List their suggestions on the board.

Then show the class the binoculars (someone may have suggested using binoculars already). Let a student use the binoculars to read the words. Say, **Blessings and Thanksgiving are the words on the paper. The words are there, but we need help to see them. These two prayers in the catechism can acts like binoculars, bringing God's blessings into focus for us.**

Table Talk

(Don't just read—TELL the following true story.)

In Eilenburg, Germany, Pastor Martin Rinckart faced the most difficult events of his life. For 19 years, armies raged around the town. Refugees continually flocked into Eilenburg, causing famine and disease. On May 8, 1637, the plague took Rinckart's beloved wife. On August 7th he conducted a funeral service for four other pastors, leaving him the only pastor in the city. Death so completely consumed the people that Rinckart often conducted funerals for 40 to 50 people a day. After conducting funerals for more than 4,480 people, the rate of death increased so quickly that the townspeople buried their dead in great trenches without waiting for a funeral service. By the end of the Thirty Years' War, nearly a third of the population had died.

Despite a life immersed in such famine and suffering, Rinckart published the famous hymn "Now Thank We All Our God." Rinckart intended this hymn as a simple prayer. He used it to bless and thank God for the meager amounts of food available during the Thirty Years' War. But today, Christians around the world sing his words in dozens of languages, thanking God for all His benefits.

Discuss one-on-one or in small groups the following questions. (Mentors will guide students through the lesson sheets.)

➡ Student material starts here.

After so much suffering, how could Pastor Rinckart write a hymn of thanks to God?

Despite his suffering, Rinckart still had God's saving grace through Christ Jesus. He had enough to support his life. He gave thanks for what he had instead of being resentful for what he did not have.

Why might God permit such suffering?

The war came because of greedy and unforgiving rulers. God may use suffering to punish the unrepentant. But suffering also comes into our lives because of persecution. As with Pastor Rinckart, God can use suffering to strengthen His people and make His glory known (e.g., John 9:1–3).

Why is it appropriate to pray the Lord's Prayer whenever we offer blessings for our food or return thanks?

The Lord's Prayer focuses on all the benefits God gives us each day.

Bible Study

Jesus leaves His home town, where many people doubt He is the Christ. Then King Herod kills Jesus' cousin, John the Baptist. Jesus leads His disciples to a quiet place for rest. Read Mark 6:30–44.

1. What does Jesus do before this meal?

He prays. Even Jesus gave thanks to the heavenly Father!

2. Though they had only five loaves of bread and two fish, what did Jesus do? See verse 41.

By God's blessing, Jesus miraculously increased the loaves and the fish. He fed the people and demonstrated that He was God's chosen servant.

3. Re-create that scene today in a large metropolitan city. Suppose there were many people with Jesus and He started to distribute bread and fish to eat. How do you think most people would react?

Answers will vary. Some might believe. Others might focus on the food as the crowd did in Jesus' day.

4. If you were one of the five thousand, what would your reaction be?

Answers will vary.

5. Recall Psalm 23:1. How does the psalmist summarize the meaning of Mark 6:42?

God satisfies our needs.

6. As you review your blessings, for what are you led to give thanks to God?

Answers will vary. Forgiveness through Christ should feature in the list.

7. Point out where the Bible story proclaims the Law and the Gospel.

For example, 6:37 describes Jesus ordering the disciples to care for the crowds. 6:34 proclaims God's mercy through Christ.

Family in Faith Journal

Parents/mentors should ask students what table prayers they typically use. Record this in the Family in Faith Journal.

Fun for Review

Prop: Paper sack (for lunch)

Characters: Zach, Sauley

Setting: The place where Jesus fed the 5,000

ZACH: There are a lot of people here.

SAULEY: Everyone wants to hear Jesus speak.

ZACH: I saw him heal a man who was deaf.

SAULEY: That's unheard of.

ZACH: Really, I saw it.

SAULEY: I watched Him give a man back his sight. The man believed Jesus could heal him.

ZACH: That's what I call blind faith!

SAULEY: He's a great teacher, too.

ZACH: It's hard to hear Him with so many people.

SAULEY: I wish someone would invent woofers and tweeters so we could hear better.

ZACH: I have a dog that woofs and a bird that tweets. How will they help?

SAULEY: Never mind.

ZACH: I'm starting to get hungry.

SAULEY: My mom packed some food.

ZACH: Whatcha got?

SAULEY: I haven't checked yet. I hope it's either peanut butter and matzo ball sandwiches or kosher pickles. *(Looks in bag)* Aw, shucks.

ZACH: Shucks? She packed some shucks?

SAULEY: No, just a couple of fish and five loaves of bread.

ZACH: Be quiet … what is that follower of Jesus asking?

(Pause while Zach and Sauley pretend to listen.)

SAULEY: He's asking if anyone has food to share.

ZACH: Offer your sack lunch.

SAULEY: I only have a little. My mom would be embarrassed for not packing enough for everyone!

ZACH: The disciple of Jesus is coming over here. I think he saw that you had food.

SAULEY: *(Looking up and speaking to disciple)* Ummm, certainly you can have my food, but it isn't much. Yes, I know the Master has need of it. Gladly I will give it to you.

ZACH: Sauley, he's giving it to Jesus. No one else had any food to share.

SAULEY: I hope my mom de-boned the fish. I don't want Jesus or His disciples to choke on my mom's fish. Oh, the guilt she'd live with if that happened.

ZACH: Listen, Jesus is blessing the food—your food. The fish and the bread.

SAULEY: He wants us to get into groups to eat. *(Looking around)* How is He going to feed this huge group? There must be some 5,000 men here, and that's not counting women and children.

ZACH: Jesus is holding up your food. He's giving thanks for it. Sauley, you're going to be famous. You would be on all the evening newscasts, if someone had invented television.

SAULEY: They are passing the food around. It looks like there's enough for everyone.

ZACH: It's a miracle. How did He do that?

SAULEY: He blessed the food and gave thanks. That's all I saw and heard.

ZACH: This Jesus is a miracle worker who knows what people need and answers them.

SAULEY: I bet my mom's food tastes even better because it was blessed by Jesus and because He gave thanks for it.

Finish the Lesson

Why do we pray before we eat? God has asked us and directed us to give thanks for the food He provides.

Does a blessing change our food or does it change us? Jesus may change our food through a blessing, as He did in the Bible story. But the blessing also serves as a reminder to us of God's kindness.

Closing Prayer

Focus the attention of the group by reciting the Table Prayers responsively.

Lesson Suggestions

Hymn: *LW* 443; *TLH* 36; *AGPS* 133
Homework: Let the students have a break or catch up on homework.
Memory Work: Table Prayers (*LSCE*, pp. 31–32)

25

Lord's Prayer, Fifth Petition

Focus on the Catechism

Focus the attention of the group by reciting the Fifth Petition of the Lord's Prayer responsively (*LSCE,* p. 19). Then pray this or a similar prayer based on the Fifth Petition:

Our Father who art in heaven, You hear our prayers despite our sins. Help us to gladly listen and have mercy when others ask us for our forgiveness; through Christ, our Lord. Amen.

Activity

Materials: Suitcase filled with books to make it as heavy as possible

Have a smaller volunteer pick up the heavy suitcase. Say, **Please hold this suitcase for me.** Ask, **How many of you have ever had to carry a heavy suitcase? What was that like?** Take time for the class to respond. Let the class watch as the student struggles to keep the suitcase off the ground.

Say, **This heavy suitcase can remind us of the burden of sin we carry. Sin weighs us down. But in the Fifth Petition we pray that our Father in heaven would not look on our sins or deny our prayers because of them.** Have a second student unload the books. The first student should now easily lift the suitcase. Say, **We deserve all the burden of sin, but Jesus takes our load. God forgives our sin for Jesus' sake.**

Table Talk

(Don't just read—TELL the following true story.)

In Papua New Guinea, a clash between two tribal groups caused 14 deaths. Following this bloody event, missionary Claudia Hansen overheard a remarkably friendly conversation between two boys in her classroom. The two boys sat together discussing the tribal fighting even though they were from the two tribes that were killing each other!

Moved by their words, Claudia asked them if they wanted to pray with her about the fighting. After they had prayed, one boy commented that they should not kill each other. Since Jesus died for them, they could forgive each other in Christ.

Discuss one-on-one or in small groups the following questions. (Mentors will guide students through the lesson sheets.)

➡ Student material starts here.

What made it possible for these two boys to sit together peacefully in class?

They believed in God's forgiveness.

Close your eyes and recall the last person you fought or argued with. In view of this story, what would you like to say to that person?

Answers should focus on God's forgiveness for that person.

Recall the worst thing that has ever happened to you. Have you forgiven the person or persons involved? Why or why not?

Answers will vary.

Bible Study

Jesus teaches His disciples to talk to the people who offend them. Peter asks how often he should forgive others. Jesus answers with a parable. Read Matthew 18:23–35.

1. As followers of Jesus, what are we called on to do? See 18:33.

Forgive as God forgives us.

2. What is the worst thing that could happen if you forgave someone who wasn't truly sorry? What's the best thing that could happen?

No one deserves forgiveness! It can't be earned. A person who wasn't truly sorry might take your forgiveness for granted. However, students should understand that when we forgive others through Christ, this relieves us of the burden of resentment.

3. In the creed we have learned that God forgives us freely through Christ. Does verse 35 mean that unless we forgive one another we may lose God's forgiveness?

The parable focuses on the king's incredible forgiveness. Every believer struggles with feelings of unforgiveness. Unforgiveness is a sin in its own right. Those who resist the Holy Spirit's call to repent of unforgiveness may fall away from Christ.

4. What do you deserve because of your sin?

Death and hell.

5. What is so amazing about God's gracious forgiveness?

He keeps on forgiving me.

6. Point out where the Bible story proclaims the Law and the Gospel.

For example, Matthew 18:25, 32–35 strongly proclaims the Law. Matthew 18:27 gently proclaims God's forgiveness.

Family in Faith Journal

Parents/mentors should describe for the students a time they struggled to forgive someone. Talk about God's forgiveness for all sins through Christ. Do not necessarily record this in the Family in Faith Journal!

Fun for Review

Props: 2 pretend microphones

Characters: Larry, the announcer; John Dibbs, a reporter; Kay Karowitz, another reporter; Mrs. Chen Selikah, the victim's mother; Ricky Riqqab, the perpetrator; Andy Dexter, someone from the public; a couple of police officers

Setting: A city street and the county jail

ANNOUNCER: We interrupt this program for this Special Report with John Dibbs. John, what do we know?

DIBBS: A terrible crime was committed in Midtown. Police won't let us get any closer, and that's just as well. It looks pretty blucky.

ANNOUNCER: Excuse me, John?

DIBBS: Awful, Larry. It looks awful. Apparently one man beat another man silly because he owed him money. And here's the really blucky part: we heard the victim shouting, "Have mercy! Have mercy!" And, by the looks of things, the attacker did not. Larry?

ANNOUNCER: I understand you have an eyewitness to this blucky event. John?

DIBBS: Larry, Mr. Andy Dexter says he knows what happened. Want to tell us what you know?

DEXTER: *(Excitedly)* OH MAN! THIS IS HORRIBLE! I CAN'T BELIEVE IT …

ANNOUNCER: John! John! Calm that man down!

DIBBS: Sir! Sir! *(Pause)* Chill.

DEXTER: Sorry! Sorry! I just can't believe it. Ricky Riqqab, that notorious, evil embezzler—you know, the one that the Governor pardoned last week?

DIBBS: Yes.

DEXTER: Well, I saw him go up to a so-called friend of his AND BEAT THAT MAN SILLY!

ANNOUNCER: Silly? This isn't funny!

DIBBS: Remember, it's an expression, Larry. And what happened next, sir?

DEXTER: It was awful! Simply awful! I could never forgive that evil Riqqab for what he did! The whole thing makes me sick. It's downright blucky, if you ask me.

DIBBS: There you have it, Larry. A truly blucky tragedy here in Midtown.

ANNOUNCER: Thank you, John. Let's go live now to reporter Kay Karowitz, who has word from the county jail. Okay, Kay, take it away!

KAROWITZ: This is scary, Larry. According to police, we're going to talk to the allegedly notorious and evil perpetrator, Richard Riqqab. And here he is now!

(POLICE bring RIQQAB up to KAROWITZ, hand-cuffed.)

KAROWITZ: Sir, you've been charged with beating a man silly! Did you indeed beat the man silly in Midtown today?

RIQQAB: I have no comment. But if I *did* have a comment, I would most likely say that he deserved it!

KAROWITZ: So you did it?

RIQQAB: If I were talking, I would say that THE LITTLE SQUIRT OWED ME MONEY! *(RIQQAB is taken away.)*

KAROWITZ: Wait! I see the mother of the victim. Excuse me, ma'am? Can we talk to you for a moment?

SELIKAH: Yes?

KAROWITZ: What is your name? Was it your son? Are you here to confront the alleged perpetrator? Do you like squash? Do you have the time? How is your son? And what is your favorite color?

SELIKAH: *(Slight pause after each answer, thinking)* Mrs. Chen Selikah. Yes … Yes … No … It's *(gives the time)* … Fine … And yellow!

ANNOUNCER: Ask if she is related to Tom Selleck.

KAROWITZ: No, Larry. Where is your son, Ma'am?

SELIKAH: He's in the hospital, but recovering well. He wanted me to come down here and tell Ricky Riqqab that my son forgives him.

KAROWITZ: WHAT?

ANNOUNCER: WHAT?

DIBBS: WHAT?

SELIKAH: *(Puzzled)* Well, yes.

KAROWITZ: Will your son still pay back the money he *allegedly* owes this *alleged* perpetrator?

SELIKAH: Of course he will. *(Walks away)*

KAROWITZ: There you have it, Larry. Truly amazing!

ANNOUNCER: I can't believe it!

Finish the Lesson

Where does the power of forgiveness come from? We can only forgive as Christ has forgiven us.

Forgiveness through Christ has been described as the teaching by which the church stands or falls. Why? Forgiveness restores our relationship with the heavenly Father. It also keeps us together as congregations in Christ.

Closing Prayer

Focus the attention of the group by reciting the Fifth Petition of the Lord's Prayer responsively (*LSCE,* p. 19). Then pray this or a similar prayer based on the Fifth Petition:

Our Father who art in heaven, You hear our prayers despite our sins. Help us to gladly listen and have mercy when others ask us for forgiveness; through Christ, our Lord. Amen.

Lesson Suggestions

Hymn: *LW* 431:1, 6; *TLH* 458; *AGPS* 96

Homework: *LSCE* questions 180–186. Have students write a summary paragraph of what they learned or answer the questions in *Exploring Luther's Small Catechism,* pages 42–43.

Memory Work: Fifth Petition; Psalm 32:5 (792); Ephesians 4:32 (795)

Lord's Prayer, Sixth and Seventh Petitions

Focus on the Catechism

Focus the attention of the group by reciting the Sixth and Seventh Petitions of the Lord's Prayer responsively (*LSCE*, pp. 19–20). Then pray this or a similar prayer based on the Sixth and Seventh Petitions:

Our Father who art in heaven, lead us in victory over the devil, the world, and our sinful nature. Rescue us when we fall and graciously take us from this valley of sorrows to Yourself in heaven. Amen.

Activity

Materials: Vacuum with an attachment hose, paper (that can be sucked up to the end of the attachment and held in place), markers, large rock with "The Word" written on it

As the students draw pictures of themselves, set the large rock on the floor before them. Collect the pictures and set one on the floor beside the rock. Say, **What will happen to the paper when the vacuum turns on?** (The vacuum will suck up the paper.) Turn on the vacuum to demonstrate. Then say, **The vacuum pulls at this paper very much like the devil, the world, and our sinful nature pull and tug at us. They tempt us and try to devour us.**

Ask, **What might rescue this paper?** (Someone will recommend the rock.) Place the rock over the remaining papers. Say, **Sometimes we might think God's ways of living and acting are a burden, like being under a rock. Maybe we feel like His Ten Commandments and His will are "crushing" us and our fun. But watch.** Turn on the vacuum. This time the paper is not sucked up. Say, **God's Word guards and anchors us. When the devil, the world, and our sinful nature try to draw us away from God, He holds us securely. Under His protection we win the victory.**

Table Talk

(Don't just read—TELL the following true story.)

It started out innocently enough. Three skiers in the French Alps—Guy McBride, Jonathan Fairley, and Paul Crowther—were looking for the quickest way down the mountain. So they passed the warning signs and headed into deeper snow. But half an hour later, the men realized their mistake. They found themselves at the top of a closed Olympic ski run, closed because it was overloaded with snow and in danger of causing an avalanche. Only minutes after rescuers guided the men off the slope, the snow tore loose and cascaded down the mountains.

Like a glimmering snowflake, temptation always seems so small. It looks so innocent, even beautiful. When we read God's warning signs, the Ten Commandments, we may think, "Certainly God is exaggerating the dangers. How could this little temptation possibly hurt me?" But soon we are up to our knees in temptation and evil. Unless God rescues us, temptation overwhelms us and buries us.

Discuss one-on-one or in small groups the following questions. (Mentors will guide students through the lesson sheets.)

➡ Student material starts here.

What evils awaited these three skiers at the end of their temptation?

Death by suffocation.

Name some snowflake-sized temptations you face.

Answers will vary.

What evil awaits you at the end of those temptations?

Allow the students to think through the larger implications of their temptations to see where sin leads.

Bible Study

Joseph's brothers sell him as a slave into Egypt. An Egyptian ruler named Potiphar buys Joseph and eventually trusts him with running his household. Read Genesis 39:1–23.

1. Considering all the things that happened to Joseph—his family's rejection, a plot to have him killed, being sold into slavery—would you have blamed him had he simply given up and surrendered to despair? Why?

No. Humanly speaking, Joseph's experiences seem overwhelming.

2. What might have happened to Joseph if he gave in to this temptation?

He never would have become the great leader that he did. He never would have saved the lives of so many people.

3. What temptations do you face daily? How are you able to resist them? Or don't you?

Answers will vary.

4. When Luther writes, "God tempts no one," what misunderstanding of the Sixth Petition is he trying to clear up?

Some might think that God actually leads or causes people to sin. Though Scripture teaches that God "tests" us, it does not teach that He provokes us to sin.

5. Have you ever been tempted in the following ways? If so, describe those times.

"Don't worry, everyone is doing it."

"It doesn't matter what you believe as long as you really believe it."

"Every religion is the same. Each one just has a little different way to heaven."

"Why do you even try … you'll never make it."

"If God didn't want you to have sex, He wouldn't have created you with the desire."

6. Read 2 Timothy 4:18. What does God promise for you in this passage?

Deliverance from every evil attack. Even if we fall into temptation, God can deliver us from evil through forgiveness in Christ.

7. How does Joseph remind you of Jesus?

Joseph trusted God, resisted temptation, and saved the lives of many.

8. Point out where the Bible story proclaims the Law and the Gospel.

For example, in Genesis 39:9 Joseph remembers God's Law. Genesis 39:23 gently proclaims God's mercy for Joseph.

Family in Faith Journal

Pair parents/mentors with each other and students with each other. Ask, "Are you more likely to give into temptation when you are with your peers or when alone?" Have students record their thoughts in the Family in Faith Journal.

Fun for Review

Characters: Monique, Erick, Monique's Thoughts, Erick's Thoughts, Teacher

Setting: School classroom. ERICK and MONIQUE are seated facing the group, taking a test. There are two chairs directly behind theirs, facing the opposite direction. Their THOUGHTS will speak from these chairs.

(Throughout the sketch ERICK continually tries to sneak a peak at MONIQUE's test. Both students should react as their THOUGHTS speak.)

ERICK'S THOUGHTS: I knew I should have studied more for this test. Monique is so smart, she probably thinks this is easy.

MONIQUE'S THOUGHTS: Wow, this is easy!

ERICK'S THOUGHTS: She's flying through those answers. I'm not even sure I spelled my name right.

MONIQUE'S THOUGHTS: This one is obviously false. That one is true.

ERICK'S THOUGHTS: I wonder if she'd notice if I took a quick peek at her answers.

MONIQUE'S THOUGHTS: This one is … hey, is Erick trying to peek at my answers.

ERICK'S THOUGHTS: Let's see, it's the true-false section. I wish I had better odds than 50–50! She writes like a girl. I can't tell if that's a "T" or an "F."

MONIQUE'S THOUGHTS: Should I let him cheat, or should I just glare at him? He's really nice, and I know he's busy with sports. Maybe I should let him see my answers.

ERICK'S THOUGHTS: I think she put "True" for the first one. Wait! I can't do this. *(Pause)* I shouldn't do this. *(Pause)* I could do this! *(Pause)* I wouldn't cheat. Would I?

MONIQUE'S THOUGHTS: What am I thinking? I worked hard to get a good grade. Besides, it's not right to let him cheat.

ERICK'S THOUGHTS: I wish our chairs weren't so close together. This is the teacher's fault. He wants to test us to see if we'll cheat.

MONIQUE'S THOUGHTS: I guess I could let him see an answer or two. He is kind of cute.

ERICK'S THOUGHTS: I wonder if she thinks I'm cute. Maybe that will be in my favor.

MONIQUE'S THOUGHTS: No! Stop it! Concentrate on your test. You're wasting time. Get back to work.

ERICK'S THOUGHTS: I'm gonna flunk this test.

MONIQUE'S THOUGHTS: I'm going to ace this test.

ERICK'S THOUGHTS: I will not cheat. I will not cheat. I will get an "F."

MONIQUE'S THOUGHTS: This essay is an easy one.

ERICK'S THOUGHTS: What's up with this essay?

(Pause)

TEACHER: Time is up. Pass your papers forward. I tried something different for this test. I mixed up the test questions so no two people sitting next to each other would be able to cheat, or if you did, you probably marked the wrong answer! I thought that might help keep you from the temptation to cheat on future tests.

ERICK'S THOUGHTS: Oh, isn't he the clever one!

MONIQUE'S THOUGHTS: Since Erick seemed to struggle on this test, maybe I will offer to help him study for the next test.

TEACHER: It's time for religion class. Everyone take out your Bibles and turn to Genesis 39. We're going to learn about someone else who was tested.

Finish the Lesson

How does cheating damage the person who cheats? You don't really learn the topic. Cheating is stealing. It is a sin against God.

How is life like a test? In life we face many difficult issues. Sometimes we fail. But God graciously cares for us and will sustain us when we face tests and temptations.

Closing Prayer

Focus the attention of the group by reciting the Sixth and Seventh Petitions of the Lord's Prayer responsively (*LSCE,* pp. 19–20). Then pray this or a similar prayer based on the Sixth and Seventh Petitions:

Our Father who art in heaven, lead us in victory over the devil, the world, and our sinful nature. Rescue us when we fall and graciously take us from this valley of sorrows to Yourself in heaven; through Christ, our Savior. Amen.

Lesson Suggestions

Hymn: *LW* 431:1, 7–8; *TLH* 458; *AGPS* 89

Homework: *LSCE* questions 228–233, 187–189. Have students write a summary paragraph of what they learned or answer the questions in *Exploring Luther's Small Catechism,* pages 52–53.

Memory Work: Sixth and Seventh Petitions; 1 Corinthians 10:12–13 (808); Revelation 21:4 (819)

Prayer upon Completing Study of the Lord's Prayer

Following the sermon, the confirmands and their parents/mentors shall come forward. They shall face the congregation, confirmands in front, parents/mentors behind. Then the minister shall say:

Beloved in the Lord, when the disciples asked our Lord Jesus Christ how they should pray, He gave them the Lord's Prayer.

The students shall then speak together the Lord's Prayer.

Let us pray for our catechumens, that our Lord God would open their hearts and the door of His mercy that they may remain faithful to Christ Jesus, our Lord:

Almighty God and Father, because You always grant growth to Your Church, increase the faith and understanding of our catechumens that, recalling the new birth by the water of Holy Baptism, they may forever continue in the family of those whom you adopt as Your sons and daughters; through Jesus Christ, our Lord.

Response: Amen.

Adapted from *Lutheran Worship*, pp. 205, 276.

Baptism and Its Benefits

Focus on the Catechism

Focus the attention of the group by reciting the first and second parts of Baptism responsively (*LSCE,* pp. 21–22). Then pray this or a similar prayer based on Baptism's benefits:

Holy Trinity—Father, Son, and Holy Spirit—You rescue us from death and the devil through the gracious washing of Baptism. Strengthen us against all doubts that we may stand against all temptations. Amen.

Activity

Have everyone, including parents/mentors, line up according to height, the shortest on the left, the tallest on the right. When everyone is in line, say, **[Name] is the shortest in the class. Does that mean [name] is less of a person than the rest of you?** (No.) Now point to the tallest person. **Does [tallest] still need God's love and forgiveness even though he/she is taller?** (Yes.) **Why?** (Before God, size doesn't matter.)

Now have everyone line up by age, youngest on the left, oldest on the right. When everyone is in line, say, **[Name] is the youngest in the class. Does that mean [name] is less of a person than the rest of you.** (No.) Now point to the oldest person. **Does [name] still need God's love and forgiveness even though he/she is older?** (Yes.) **Why?** (Before God, age doesn't matter.)

Say, **Some people are confused about Baptism. They imagine that size and age are important to God, that you can't get baptized until you reach a certain size or age. But the Bible never teaches that you need to be a certain size or age to get baptized. Everyone is a sinner. Everyone needs God's forgiveness in Baptism.**

Table Talk

(Don't just read—TELL the following true story.)

Though every country has its own set of laws, certain laws appear everywhere. One of the most basic rights recognized throughout the world is the right of a child, even an infant, to inherit its parents' property.

For example, when Christina Onassis died in 1998, she left 200 billion dollars to her daughter, Athina. Even though Athina was only 12 years old at the time, she had the right to inherit her mother's vast fortune.

But history also provides even more remarkable examples. In September 1422, Henry VI inherited the entire kingdom of England from his father even though Henry was only eight months old! Two months later baby Henry inherited his grandfather's kingdom in France. Though Henry VI was only a baby, no one disputed his right to inherit these kingdoms from his father and grandfather. That's because inheritance does not depend upon the age or ability of the one who receives it. Inheritance depends on the generosity of the person who gives it.

Discuss one-on-one or in small groups the following questions. (Mentors will guide students through the lesson sheets.)

➡ <u>Student material starts here.</u>

The Bible compares salvation to an inheritance (Titus 3:7). How might this help you understand Baptism for infants? for mentally handicapped people?

If salvation works like an inheritance, then God gives it freely through Christ.

Is God limited by our weakness or lack of understanding? Explain your answer.

No. Our weaknesses do not limit God. His mighty power called the world into existence. He can save us.

Read the second paragraph under the third article of the creed (p. 15). How might this help you understand Baptism for infants as well as adults?

No one has the power to believe unless the Holy Spirit calls him/her to faith. See Ephesians 2:1–5, 8–9.

Bible Study

Jesus' last recorded words in Matthew echo the command He gives to each and every one of us—to make disciples. In His command He tells us how to specifically do it. Read Matthew 28:16–20.

1. According to Jesus, what two actions make disciples? See 28:19–20.

Baptizing and teaching.

2. In what way are our parents following these instructions by placing us in confirmation classes?

We are learning the teachings of Jesus.

3. When Jesus says, "all nations," what age groups does that include for Baptism?

"All nations" means all people regardless of age.

4. If people in other countries have their own religions, why would Jesus tell His followers to make disciples of all nations?

Because Jesus is the only true Savior.

5. Talk about a Baptism you've seen in church. What happened? Who gave the church the right to baptize?

Answers will vary. The right to baptize comes from Jesus Himself.

6. Was the Baptism that of an infant? Who said he/she even wanted to be baptized?

Parents or guardians bring a child for Baptism. Just as they act on the child's behalf in other matters, they do the same in Baptism.

7. A Baptist friend in school says your religion is wrong because you believe that infants should be baptized. How would you explain or defend the practice of your church?

Answers will vary.

8. Point out where the story proclaims the Law and the Gospel.

For example, 28:17b tells us that some of the apostles doubted. 28:20b proclaims the promise that Christ is with us always.

Family in Faith Journal

Parents/mentors should describe a time when they faced death, injury, or destruction. How did they get through it? How did God help? Record the events in the Family in Faith Journal.

Fun for Review

Characters: Suzy, Billy, Bobby, Amy

Setting: Outside of class talking about Baptism

SUZY: I still can't believe your parents didn't have you baptized when you were a baby, Billy.

BILLY: They just didn't, okay?

BOBBY: Hey, that's okay. You're getting baptized before Confirmation Day, and I think that's great!

AMY: I think it makes more sense to wait until you're older anyway.

BOBBY: What?

SUZY: You do?

AMY: Sure. Billy will be able to remember his Baptism Day. Right? Can any of you remember the day you were baptized?

BOBBY: I was three weeks old. If I could remember, that would be a little scary.

SUZY: I can't remember, but I've seen pictures!

AMY: My mom said I threw up all over the pastor's robe. I certainly don't remember that, and it's just as well. Now, if I had been older, then that wouldn't have happened, right?

BOBBY: That's not the point, Amy. You were baptized as an infant, I was, and Suzy was because our parents were following Christ's command to go and baptize all nations. That includes babies, children, and adults.

AMY: Yeah, but I still think it makes sense to wait, so the person being baptized can really appreciate their Baptism.

BOBBY: I do appreciate my Baptism, *thank you*.

SUZY: Are you looking forward to Sunday, Billy?

BILLY: Yeah, sort of.

BOBBY: Sort of? This is going to be awesome!

AMY: There, you see! It's going to be awesome—and even more awesome because Billy will be able to remember its awesomeness. Right, Billy-boy?

BILLY: I suppose.

BOBBY: I think you're mixing up what is really important here. If you remember your Baptism because you were older, wonderful. But what really matters is that God remembers! And He does. Baptism is something God is doing for you, not the other way around.

AMY: Yeah, but a baby can't recognize that this is something God is doing. So how can a baby appreciate it?

SUZY: Oooo, good question, *Aim*. Answer that one, Robert!

BOBBY: Let me put it this way. When a baby is born, do you think that baby recognizes her daddy?

AMY: No. She's just an infant.

BOBBY: Exactly. But just because the baby doesn't recognize her daddy, does that make him any less her daddy?

AMY: I guess not.

BOBBY: Of course it doesn't! Parents don't wait until their children can call them by name before they declare themselves to be the parents!

BILLY: What's your point, *Pastor* Bob?

BOBBY: Very funny. My point is this: the benefits of Baptism come from God—His Word connected with the water! Through Baptism God gives the gift of faith to the child. It is a gift, not a reward for being someone special or smart or whatever. Baptism is "grace given," not a "wage earned"!

SUZY: So, Billy, I guess you're not so special after all. See? Told you so.

BILLY: Ha-ha, Suze. So does this mean that I'm not God's child until I get baptized? Does this mean I don't have His grace until Sunday?

Finish the Lesson

What's the most important thing to remember about Baptism? Baptism personally applies the benefits of Jesus' death and resurrection for our salvation.

Does Billy have God's grace even though he's not yet baptized? How? Yes. He has heard and believes God's Word. The Holy Spirit also applies the benefits of Jesus' death and resurrection through the Word.

Closing Prayer

Focus the attention of the group by reciting the first and second parts of Baptism responsively (*LSCE*, pp. 21-22). Then pray this or a similar prayer based on Baptism's benefits:

Holy Trinity—Father, Son, and Holy Spirit—You rescue us from death and the devil through the gracious washing of Baptism. Strengthen us against all doubts that we may stand against all temptations. Forgive us when we fall; through Christ, our Savior. Amen.

Lesson Suggestions

Hymn: *LW* 223:1-4; *TLH* 226; *AGPS* 77

Homework: *LSCE* questions 239-247. Have students write a summary paragraph of what they learned or answer the questions in *Exploring Luther's Small Catechism,* pages 54-55.

Memory Work: Baptism, Part 1 and Part 2; Acts 2:38-39 (835); John 3:5-6 (841)

How Baptism Works

Focus on the Catechism

Focus the attention of the group by reciting the third part of Baptism responsively (*LSCE*, p. 22). Then pray this or a similar prayer based on how Baptism works:

Holy Trinity—Father, Son, and Holy Spirit—through Baptism You wash us and renew us by the Holy Spirit. Make us worthy heirs of Your kingdom this day and every day. Amen.

Activity

Materials: Several packages of instant pudding, milk to prepare pudding, hand mixer or whisk

Fill a bowl with the dry pudding mix. Say, **This powder is not what we would call pudding. It has the potential of being pudding, but right now it is just powder. What does this pudding need?** (Milk.) Pour in the milk. Say, **Now is it pudding?** (No. The milk needs to be mixed in with the powder.)

Say, **We won't have pudding until we mix the milk with the powder. In a similar way, Baptism requires ingredients and mixing. The ingredients for a Baptism are water and God's Word. When we wash someone "in the name of the Father, and of the Son, and of the Holy Spirit," we have a Baptism. The two ingredients come together to create the miracle of Baptism.** Use an electric hand mixer to quickly mix the pudding and milk. Plan for time to enjoy the pudding at the end of the lesson. Say, **Today we will learn how Baptism works.**

Table Talk

(Don't just read—TELL the following true story.)

From 1976 to 1981, Argentina's dictator, Jorge Videla, committed an amazing crime. Videla ordered the arrest of everyone who opposed him, including hundreds of pregnant women. Videla's prison doctors led these pregnant women blindfolded and handcuffed into the birthing rooms. After the women gave birth, the doctors immediately took the children away and gave them to friends of the dictator. Instead of inheriting their parents' life and values, these children were raised by the enemy, unaware of who their true parents were!

In a similar way, the Bible warns that every person—including you and me—is born into the clutches of our chief enemy, the devil. Like a vile dictator, the devil enslaves us in our sins and robs us of our inheritance as the children of God. Unless we are born again and become heirs of God's kingdom, we remain imprisoned under the devil's rule.

Discuss one-on-one or in small groups the following questions. (Mentors will guide students through the lesson sheets.)

➡ Student material starts here.

How does Baptism take us out of the devil's kingdom and bring us into God's kingdom?

Through Baptism we become heirs of God and members of His kingdom.

Are all people God's children by birth? Explain.

All people are born under the slavery of sin and the power of the devil. They need to be set free. That is why God gave us Baptism and His Word.

Bible Study

Acts 2 gives us a picture of the newborn church, how it was formed and what it looked like once it came into existence. Those who were baptized looked and acted totally differently than they did before their conversion. Read Acts 2:22–47.

1. When Peter gives his sermon, what themes does he focus on?

The death and resurrection of Jesus Christ as a fulfillment of God's promises.

2. What new promise does Peter proclaim in verses 38–39?

The promise of forgiveness and the Holy Spirit.

3. How does God fulfill this promise to His people?

Through Baptism.

4. Once baptized, what was extraordinary about the way the believers lived? See Acts 2:42–47.

They devoted themselves to the apostles' teaching, fellowship, and prayer. God blessed them with miracles. They shared freely with one another and had great joy and sincerity.

5. Name someone in your life who truly lives out his/her Christian faith. What does he/she do that makes him/her extraordinary?

Answers will vary.

6. According to Mark 16:16, what condemns a person (see *LSCE*, p. 22)?

Unbelief condemns. Those who trust in Christ but have not yet been baptized should be regarded as God's people by faith.

7. If you are baptized, what comfort or encouragement does that provide for you?

Answers will vary. However, each student should understand that Baptism makes him/her a child of God, an inheritor of His blessings.

8. Point out where the story proclaims the Law and the Gospel.

For example, 2:23 condemns the people for condemning Jesus. 2:24–28 proclaims how the Father raised Jesus up to be the Savior.

Family in Faith Journal

From parents or church records, learn the baptismal date and sponsors for the students. Record them in the Family in Faith Journal.

Fun for Review

Prop: Notebook

Characters: Tommy, Mom

Setting: Their home

MOM: So how was school today?

TOMMY: Fine.

MOM: That's what you always say. Tell me something you learned today.

TOMMY: I dunno. I learned math in math class and English in English class.

MOM: What did you learn in confirmation class today? And don't say, "I learned confirmation in confirmation class." That doesn't work.

TOMMY: Oh, I did learn something cool today. I found out a way to tell which adults are baptized and which aren't just by looking at them.

MOM: What? You're telling me that you can tell who is baptized by looking at them?

TOMMY: Yep. Like Mr. Parlidge. I can tell he's not baptized.

MOM: You're kidding. I'm sure he is.

TOMMY: Not according to what I learned in class today.

MOM: I can't believe Pastor would tell you that.

TOMMY: He didn't mention Mr. Parlidge by name, but I know he isn't baptized because of what Pastor taught us today about Baptism.

MOM: I'm confused.

TOMMY: I don't think Mr. Ewing, Mr. Rodriguez, or even Mrs. Sardis are baptized!

MOM: Now come on. Mr. Ewing is one of the elders at church. He's baptized. Mr. Rodriguez teaches the adult Bible class. He even taught a class on Baptism. You're just trying to get me to stop asking you what you learned in school every day.

TOMMY: I'm telling the truth, Mom.

MOM: Okay, tell me exactly what you talked about today in confirmation class. What did Pastor teach you?

TOMMY: He told us that our hair is made through Baptism.

MOM: What?

TOMMY: I thought about the last baby I saw baptized. She didn't have any hair, but I noticed last week in church her hair was growing.

MOM: And what about Mr. Parlidge, Mr. Ewing, Mr. Rodriguez, and Mrs. Sardis?

TOMMY: Haven't you noticed they're all bald?

MOM: Mrs. Sardis isn't bald!

TOMMY: Well, she's awfully close to bald! Mr. Sardis has more hair than she does!

MOM: This still doesn't make sense. Now you said Pastor told you that our hair is made through Baptism?

TOMMY: I'm sure he did. At least I'm pretty sure. Look, here are my notes. *(Hands notebook to MOM)*

MOM *(Reading notes)* You wrote down, "We are made hairs through Baptism." *(Starts to laugh)* Tommy! Pastor said, "We are made **heirs,** not **hairs** through Baptism"!

TOMMY: Oops. What does heirs mean?

MOM: An heir is someone who gets an inheritance. Through our Baptism we are heirs of forgiveness, salvation, and all of God's incredible gifts. That's all part of our inheritance because we are children of God through Baptism.

TOMMY: I guess that makes a lot of difference.

MOM: I think you better listen more closely in class. And ask questions if you don't understand!

TOMMY: I think so too!

MOM: It's time for bed. Go take your shower first … and wash your hair, you heir of salvation through Baptism!

TOMMY: Very funny, Mom!

Finish the Lesson

What's the purpose of Baptism? To keep you out of hell! Baptism washes away our sins and makes us children of God.

What do we inherit through Baptism? Eternal life and a peace with our heavenly Father.

Closing Prayer

Focus the attention of the group by reciting the third part of Baptism responsively (*LSCE,* p. 22). Then pray this or a similar prayer based on how Baptism works:

Holy Trinity—Father, Son, and Holy Spirit—through Baptism You wash us and renew us by the Holy Spirit. Make us worthy heirs of Your kingdom this day and every day. Forgive us when we stumble. Amen.

Lesson Suggestions

Hymn: *LW* 223:5-7; *TLH* 298; *AGPS* 132

Homework: *LSCE* questions 248–254. Have students write a summary paragraph of what they learned or answer the questions in *Exploring Luther's Small Catechism,* page 55.

Memory Work: Baptism, Part 3; 1 Peter 3:21 (852); Romans 6:6 (865)

Baptismal Life

Focus on the Catechism

Focus the attention of the group by reciting the fourth part of Baptism responsively (*LSCE,* pp. 22–23). Then pray this or a similar prayer based on what Baptism indicates:

Holy Trinity—Father, Son, and Holy Spirit—You call us to repentance and new life each day. Drown all sin and evil desires within us so that we live in righteousness and purity. For You live and reign forever, one God. Amen.

Activity

Materials: Pair of clean white socks, pair of very dirty white socks

Hold up the dirty pair of socks. Ask, **If you found this pair of socks in your drawer, would you wear them to school?** Most students will say no. Ask them why they would not wear this pair of socks. **Do you think the socks should be thrown out?** (Some might say yes, because they are so dirty.) Ask, **Do you always throw out your clothes after you wear them?** (The students will realize the socks can be washed.) Suggest to the students that the socks could be washed in hot water with bleach. The washing would make them clean and again fit for wearing.

Hold up the clean pair of socks. Say, **These socks have been washed and they are ready to wear. Luther explained Christian life as a daily return to the washing of Baptism. He taught that daily we are to remember that sin makes us dirty, like the other socks, but through Baptism Jesus makes us clean, like these socks. Daily through contrition and repentance we drown our sins and evil desires. It is like putting dirty socks in the washing machine. When you pull them out, they are clean again. Daily repenting of our sins and remembering our Baptism is like coming out of the washer and dryer clean and ready for another day living for God in righteousness and purity.**

Table Talk

(Don't just read—TELL the following true story.)

When Louis IX was only 12 years old, France crowned him as its king at the city of Rheims. Though Louis was tall, stately, and mature for his age, he trembled as the crown was lowered onto his head. Louis understood what a vast territory he would rule. He knew that other leaders in France opposed his kingship. Because he was so inexperienced, he had agreed to submit to his counselors before he made decisions.

But when the coronation ceremony proclaimed him "Louis of Rheims" according to the custom of the day, the young man immediately protested. He insisted that the people call him "Louis of Poissy" because Poissy was the city where he was baptized. When challenged to lead his entire nation, Louis's heart clung to the one blessing that he knew he could count on, the blessing that could never be taken away from him: his Baptism. He recalled how God placed His blessing upon him in Baptism and guided him from that day forward.

Discuss one-on-one or in small groups the following questions. (Mentors will guide students through the lesson sheets.)

➡️ Student material starts here.

Why was Louis' Baptism so important to him?

Because in Baptism God gave Louis the gift he could count on—salvation and eternal life in Christ. Baptismal faith receives and lives in these certain promises from God.

In the lesson on daily prayers Luther encouraged us to make the sign of the cross each day. How does that practice fit with this part of the catechism on Baptism?

The sign of the cross reminds us of our Baptism in God's name. Luther encourages us to return to that promise daily.

Bible Study

After a group of Pharisees ask Jesus about the coming of the kingdom of God, He tells a series of parables about daily Christian life. Read Luke 18:9–14.

1. Though both men came to the temple, what was the problem with the Pharisee?

He placed his hope of forgiveness on what he did as opposed to what Jesus Christ did for him.

2. If you had been a Pharisee listening to this parable, how do you think you'd have felt about what Jesus said? Convicted? Angry? Uneasy?

Answers will vary.

3. What made the tax collector's confession acceptable before God? See also Psalm 51:16–17.

The tax collector's confession was contrite. He was truly sorry.

4. Put Luke 18:14 into your own words.

Answers will vary.

5. Define the words "righteousness" and "justified."

Righteousness might be defined as "being right with God" and "justified" as "God treats me just as if I'd never done anything wrong."

6. Complete the following sentence: Because of Baptism, I know I am …

7. How do you continue to drown the Old Adam within?

Through daily contrition and repentance.

8. What's the biggest change in you because of Jesus?

Through faith in Jesus Christ one is reconnected to God. A relationship has been reestablished.

9. Point out where the story proclaims the Law and the Gospel.

For example, in 18:14 Jesus condemns the false righteousness of the Pharisee and declares the tax collector justified or forgiven by God's mercy.

Family in Faith Journal

Parents/mentors should tell the students about a time when they were tempted to give up. Discuss the hope and strength provided by Christ in such moments. Have the students record that experience in the Family in Faith Journal.

Fun for Review

Prop: Bible

Characters: Person, Good Angel, Evil Angel

Setting: A path or row through the room. EVIL ANGEL stands at one end, GOOD ANGEL at the other.

(PERSON starts down the path toward EVIL ANGEL.)

EVIL ANGEL: Hey, righteous dude! You're on the right path! Keep a comin'! You won't get hurt. This is the way of the day!

GOOD ANGEL: Stop! Wait!

EVIL ANGEL: Butt out, fly-boy! This one's mine!

GOOD ANGEL: Fight the temptation! You're going to get hurt!

PERSON: Well, I know I shouldn't be here.

EVIL ANGEL: Yes, you should! Yes, you should!

GOOD ANGEL: That's right. Say it to the Lord. Talk to Him—He will turn you around. Remember who you are.

PERSON: I'm rotten. That's what I am. I guess this is where I actually belong.

EVIL ANGEL: Bingo!

PERSON: I know I shouldn't be here; but what does it matter? I've done so much to the Lord! Why should He ever forgive someone like me?

EVIL ANGEL: Good question, young lad. Come here, and we'll talk about it.

GOOD ANGEL: Remember who you are. Remember whose name you bear!

EVIL ANGEL: Like he can hear you.

GOOD ANGEL: Or you, for that matter.

EVIL ANGEL: Hey! At least he's on my path! It's in the bag; give it up!

PERSON: *(Falls to his knees to pray)* O Lord, be merciful to me, a sinner! *(Arises and brushes himself off)*

EVIL ANGEL: That's alright! Come on down, let's get touched by an angel. Hey! What's he doing? Where's he going? *(PERSON starts to walk in the opposite direction.)*

GOOD ANGEL: It's called repentance. The Lord changed his heart.

(GOOD ANGEL pushes a Bible in front of PERSON.)

EVIL ANGEL: Hey! You can't do that! That's not fair!

PERSON: *(Picking up the Bible)* Here it is! Thank You, Lord! "For all have sinned and fall short of the glory of God, and are justified freely by His grace through the redemption that came by Christ Jesus" (Romans 3:23–24). And what was my confirmation verse? Oh, yeah, how could I forget? "Be faithful, even to the point of death, and I will give you the crown of life" (Revelation 2:10).

EVIL ANGEL: That's it! I'm outta here! But I'll be back!

GOOD ANGEL: And I'll be waiting.

(EVIL ANGEL exits. GOOD ANGEL exits with PERSON.)

Finish the Lesson

Who was at work in the person's life to turn him/her in repentance? The Holy Spirit.

What purpose does the Bible serve in daily life? With repentant hearts, we return to our Baptism daily. Since the Spirit has sealed us in Baptism, it is always there for us.

Closing Prayer

Focus the attention of the group by reciting the fourth part of Baptism responsively (*LSCE*, pp. 22–23). Then pray this or a similar prayer based on what Baptism indicates:

Holy Trinity—Father, Son, and Holy Spirit—You call us to repentance and new life each day. Drown all sins and evil desires within us so that we live in righteousness and purity. For You live and reign forever, one God. Amen.

Lesson Suggestions

Hymn: *LW* 437; *TLH* 23; *AGPS* 269

Homework: *LSCE* questions 255–260. Have students write a summary paragraph of what they learned or answer the questions in *Exploring Luther's Small Catechism,* page 56.

Memory work: Baptism, Part 4; Ephesians 4:24 (871); Romans 6:3–4 (872)

Prayer upon Completing Study of Baptism

Following the sermon, the confirmands and their parents/mentors shall come forward. They shall face the congregation, confirmands in front, parents/mentors behind. Then the minister shall say:

Beloved in the Lord, after Jesus rose from the dead, He gathered the eleven disciples in Galilee and taught them to baptize.

The students shall then speak together the words of Baptism.

Let us pray for our catechumens, that our Lord God would open their hearts and the door of His mercy that they may remain faithful to Christ Jesus, our Lord:

Almighty God and Father, because You always grant growth to Your Church, increase the faith and understanding of our catechumens that, recalling the new birth by the water of Holy Baptism, they may forever continue in the family of those whom You adopt as Your sons and daughters; through Jesus Christ, our Lord.

Response: Amen.

Adapted from *Lutheran Worship*, pp. 205, 276.

Confession and Absolution

Focus on the Catechism

Focus the attention of the group by reciting the definition of confession responsively (*LSCE,* p. 24). Then pray this or a similar prayer based on the definition of confession:

Merciful Savior, You promise complete forgiveness for all my sins. Help me to confess my sins in complete confidence that You will forgive me. Help me trust the forgiveness and counsel You speak through the pastor; for You live and reign with the Father and the Spirit, one God now and forever. Amen.

Activity

Materials: 6 to 10 belts to bind 2 students together

As in lesson 11, strap two students so they can't get loose. Say, **Sin binds us and makes us helpless.** Now have a third volunteer release one of them. Tell the free person to release the other. Say, **In confession and Absolution we use the power of God's forgiveness to free one another. When you hear the word "absolution," think of the word "loose," because it's about God setting us loose from our sins through the merits of Christ.**

Table Talk

(Don't just read—TELL the following true story.)

We tend to think of slavery as a thing of the past. But in the North African nation of Sudan, you can buy a child for about $63. Since 1983, Muslim raiders from the northern part of the country have been enslaving children from the southern part of the country and selling them. Some of these children have grown up in slavery. They can only pray each day that they will someday experience freedom.

While we should certainly pray for these children and seek their release, we must also remember that physical slavery is not the only form of slavery afflicting people today. The Bible teaches that sin enslaves every one of us from the beginning of life. Unless God releases us from our sins, we are condemned to a life of bondage.

Discuss one-on-one or in small groups the following questions. (Mentors will guide students through the lesson sheets.)

➡ <u>Student material starts here.</u>

What most shocks you about today's true story?

That slavery still exists.

What kind of slavery does each of us experience?

Every one of us is born a slave to sin.

How do we receive freedom?

Christ frees us through Baptism or His Word of Absolution, the Gospel.

Bible Study

Early in His ministry Jesus heals many who are sick. He attracts huge crowds. Read Luke 5:17–26.

1. What might the people have thought was the most immediate need of the paralyzed man?

Physical healing.

2. What did Jesus see as the man's most immediate need?

Forgiveness.

3. In what way are we similar to the paralyzed man?

The paralyzed man, like everyone else, had sinned. The consequence of sin is death (Romans 6:23).

4. Though the people were impressed with the physical healing of the paralyzed man, what is even more amazing about the spiritual healing that took place?

Through forgiveness, Christ gave the man the gift of eternal life and freedom from the oppression of the devil.

5. How does Jesus forgive our sins daily?

When we ask forgiveness by remembering our Baptism, calling on Him in the Lord's Prayer, or when someone else shares the Gospel with us.

6. What happens when we acknowledge our sins and confess them before God? before one another?

God frees us and unites us with Himself and fellow believers.

7. Who in the world or in heaven gives anyone the right to forgive another person? See Matthew 18:18 and John 20:23 if you need help.

God alone has the right to forgive sins, but He authorizes and empowers us to do the same through the Gospel.

8. In what ways might the courts of our land be filled with fewer lawsuits if we practiced the art of confession and absolution more? How might the practice of confession and absolution keep more marriages together?

If people readily practiced forgiveness, there would be greater peace and harmony.

9. Point out where the Bible story proclaims the Law and the Gospel.

For example, in Luke 5:22 Jesus rebukes the Pharisees. In Luke 5:24 Jesus declares the paralytic forgiven.

Family in Faith Journal

Have students complete this sentence: When I admit I've done wrong ... Parents/mentors should record the students' comments in the Family in Faith Journal.

Fun for Review

Characters: DJ, Station Manager

Setting: Radio station studio

DJ: *(On air)* Would you like to shed a few extra pounds? Does your midsection need some strengthening? Gotta lotta love in your love handles? If you're looking for a solution to help with your midsection abs, you need to know about Ab Solution. For tighter, firmer abs, you need to get the Ab Solution! This sounds like something I can use, so I'm going to be checking into it this week and letting you know more about it. For more info, try dialing 1-A-B-S-O-L-U-T-I-O-N. Ask for Luke at extension 5-17-26. You're listening to KCIN. And here's the news …

(Takes headphones off and sits back in chair)

STATION MANAGER: *(Entering the studio)* What was that?

DJ: What?

STATION MANAGER: The Ab Solution—for tighter, firmer abs, you need to get Ab Solution!

DJ: I wasn't joking around. I was ab-libbing; I mean *ad*-libbing! I found this note on the console. I thought it was from one of our sponsors, so I put it on the air.

STATION MANAGER: This is a free public-service announcement. It's from the church—my church—down the street. It says that on the back of the paper.

DJ: What's a church doing selling body-building equipment?

STATION MANAGER: They aren't. They asked us to promote a public discussion on Absolution.

DJ: Absolution? You mean one word? It's not 'AB'… 'SOLUTION'? *(Pointing to tummy)*

STATION MANAGER: No.

DJ: So what is Absolution?

STATION MANAGER: It's another word for 'forgive-

ness.' We confess our sins and receive Absolution—forgiveness. I guess in a way it *is* a body-building power. Confessing our sins and receiving God's forgiveness builds up the body of Christ.

DJ: I'm sorry for messing this up, boss.

STATION MANAGER: You're forgiven!

DJ: My sin has been absolved! Cool!

STATION MANAGER: I guess you weren't so far off. People need to shed a few extra pounds of sin and guilt—Absolution is the way! And Absolution strengthens the body of Christ and our spiritual bodies. And for God to forgive us, He's gotta lotta love through His Son, Jesus!

DJ: I knew it all the time!

STATION MANAGER: The news is almost over.

DJ: But what's up with this Luke guy I told them to ask for?

STATION MANAGER: Luke is a book in the Bible, chapter 5, verses 17–26. That's the story the church is using to discuss the topic. I'll show you when you're off the air.

DJ: Sounds good. The news is over and I'm on! *(Puts headphones on and turns up the volume—is on the air)* Thanks for joining me this afternoon. Before we get back to the music, I have to apologize about the Ab Solution commercial. Here's the real story: You see, it's not about body building …

Finish the Lesson

What is Absolution? Forgiveness through Christ, loosing us from all our sins.

When do you receive Absolution? After the general confession in the Divine Service. You can also seek Absolution privately from your pastor.

Closing Prayer

Focus the attention of the group by reciting the definition of confession responsively (*LSCE*, p. 24). Then pray this or a similar prayer based on the definition of confession:

Merciful Savior, You promise complete forgiveness for all my sins. Help me to confess my sins in complete confidence that You will forgive me. Help me trust the forgiveness and counsel You speak through the pastor; for You live and reign with the Father and the Spirit, one God now and forever. Amen.

Lesson Suggestions

Hymn: *LW* 230:1–2; *TLH* 329; *AGPS* 249

Homework: *LSCE* questions 261–268. Have students write a summary paragraph of what they learned or answer the questions in *Exploring Luther's Small Catechism,* pages 56–7, part D.

Memory Work: "What is Confession?"; James 5:16 (882); Psalm 103:12 (887)

31 Guilt and Peace

Focus on the Catechism

Focus the attention of the group by reciting "What sins should we confess?" responsively (*LSCE,* p. 24). Then pray this or a similar prayer based on the definition of confession:

Merciful Savior, sometimes after I confess my sins I still feel guilty. Through my pastor and the mutual encouragement of other Christians, grant me Your forgiveness. For you live and reign with the Father and the Holy Spirit, one God now and forever. Amen.

Activity

Materials: Vinegar, baking soda, 2 containers with snap-on lids

Say, **If there is a heart that feels its sin and desires consolation, it has in confession and Absolution a sure refuge when it hears in God's Word that God looses and absolves sins. We must understand that sin and guilt create pressure within us. People can only hold sin and guilt inside for so long before they begin to feel torn apart by it. God has given us confession and Absolution to relieve and remove the pressure of guilt and fear that sin causes. Let me demonstrate.**

Let's say this container represents you and me. This vinegar is our sin. Pour the vinegar into a container. Say, **We are filled with sin. Now I will add the guilt and fear that come as a result of sin.** Put in the baking soda. Quickly snap the top on the container. Let the class watch the pressure build. The top will pop off the container. Say, **Sin, fear, and guilt act the same way in us. They tear us apart so that we cannot experience the peace that God desires for His children. We are constantly under pressure to try to hide the sin, guilt, and fear. However, through confession and Absolution Christ forgives us and leads us to peace.**

Let's try this again. Repeat the demonstration using the second container. However, before the top pops off, open it slightly and release the pressure. Continue to release the pressure until the chemical reaction has stopped. Say, **God gave us confession and Absolution to remove the guilt and fear of sin from our lives. It is a way of removing the pressure we feel, granting us the forgiveness Christ earned for us on the cross and comforting us with His peace.**

Table Talk

(Don't just read—TELL the following true story.)

When an accident in a coal mine near Scranton, Pennsylvania, left several miners trapped, a crowd gathered outside the mine. As the rescue efforts dragged on for hours and days, the waiting crowd began to lose patience. Many of them were convinced that the owners of the mine had neglected the mines and thereby had caused the accident. Angry people began to threaten harm to the mine owners as a way of avenging the trapped men.

Just as it seemed likely that a riot would break out, an eleven-year-old girl began to sing. At first she could barely get the words out, she felt so frightened by the crowd. But as she sang, she gained confidence and grew louder and louder. The crowd grew silent as her song confessed her helplessness and need for God's strength. Others then joined her in singing. The song that quieted the crowd and assured them of God's love and protection in that hour of distress was the classic hymn of the Reformation, "A Mighty Fortress Is Our God."

Discuss one-on-one or in small groups the following questions. (Mentors will guide students through the lesson sheets.)

➡ Student material starts here.

How might you have reacted if your father or your brother were trapped in the mine?

Probably frightened or angry.

How did the singing of "A Mighty Fortress" calm the crowd?

The song reminded the people that their hope was in God. He alone could grant them peace in that hour.

Do you have a song or hymn that could comfort you in a similar situation?

Answers will vary. Comment especially on how the hymn assures you of your Savior's love and forgiveness.

Bible Study

After a discussion of greatness in the kingdom of heaven, Jesus turns to the topic of sin, guilt, and forgiveness. Read Matthew 18:10–20.

1. What does Jesus' teaching tell us about the importance of forgiveness? Choose a verse that proves your point.

Forgiveness is all important. Love drives God to seek the lost and forgive them. It causes us to carefully seek reconciliation with our brethren. Forgiveness through Christ (justification) is the central teaching of the Christian faith.

2. How does it feel when, after you've done something wrong to another person, you ask for forgiveness and the person hugs you or shakes your hand and says, "Of course, I forgive you"? Can you give an example of when this has happened to you?

Answers will vary.

3. If guilt is defined as "the awareness of having done something wrong" and peace as "inner contentment," why would the reality and consolation of forgiveness bring about peace and freedom from guilt?

Forgiveness removes all guilt and sets things right. Forgiveness restores broken relationships.

4. Though we know we have forgiveness from God, in what way might it be beneficial to receive that forgiveness and consolation privately from a pastor?

At times our conscience so greatly plagues us that we have trouble believing God's forgiveness. The pastor is God's special servant to speak His Word of peace.

5. Point out where the Bible story proclaims the Law and the Gospel.

For example, 18:10 warns us not to look down on other believers. Matthew 18:14 tells us how God wants to save His people.

Family in Faith Journal

Students and their parents/mentors should consider what they might ask the pastor to help them with. What things wouldn't they ask him to help them with? Record these thoughts in the Family in Faith Journal.

Fun for Review

Prop: Shepherd's rod (just use a yardstick)

Characters: 5 Sheep, Shepherd, someone to make wolf sounds

Setting: A pasture where SHEEP 2-5 are grazing and bleating

SHEEP 2–5: Baaaa! Baaaa! Baaaa! Baaaa!

SHEPHERD: Hello, sheep. What's all the fuss? What's the matter? Let's see now, I need to get a count.

(He looks out into imaginary pasture and uses the rod to count the sheep.)

SHEPHERD: Ninety-six. Ninety-seven. Ninety-eight. Ninety-nine. And … wait a minute! Oh, no! *(SHEEP get restless.)* I had a hundred sheep! Where's the other … ?

(SHEPHERD exits.)

SHEEP 2: Oh, there he goes. Poor master …

SHEEP 3: This makes no sense! It's only ONE sheep. There's ninety-nine of us left!

SHEEP 4: That rotten sheep doesn't even deserve the master's energy.

SHEEP 5: Now, now. He knows what he's doing. Each of us is equally important to the master.

(SHEEP 1 wanders aimlessly and scared. Wolf sounds in the background.)

SHEEP 1: Oh, this is *baaaad*! This was not a very good idea. What was that? I'm so scared. I know I shouldn't have left. I know I shouldn't have said those things to my wooly friends. Oh, I wish I were back in the green pastures near the still water! Oh, I'm lost … what was that? Who's out there?

(SHEEP 1 sits on the floor, curled up, sobbing. SHEPHERD arrives and immediately goes to SHEEP 1. He kneels down and rubs SHEEP 1's back.)

SHEPHERD: Oh, foolish sheep. Why did you leave me? You could have been killed. You were lost, but now you are found. I should put you on my shoulders and carry you home … but you look like you've put on a few pounds. You'll just have to follow me. Let's go! *(SHEEP 1 follows SHEPHERD. Cut back to the pasture.)*

SHEPHERD: Look! My sheep. I have found him!

SHEEP: *(Looking up in amazement)* Baaaa! Baaaa! Baaaa! Baaaa!

(SHEPHERD leaves. He locks the gate.)

SHEEP 2: So how was your great day of independence?

SHEEP 3: Yeah, why did you come *baaaack*?

SHEEP 1: That was a pretty dumb thing to do, fellas. I should never have left.

SHEEP 2: We forgive you.

SHEEP 1: You don't know how glad I am to hear you say that in person! If the master wouldn't have come for me, I would have never found my way back. I was in *saaaad* shape thinking I would never see any of you again—and never get to tell you I was sorry.

SHEEP 5: We're glad you're *baaaaack*! Right, everyone?

ALL SHEEP: *Baaaack! Baaaack! Baaaack!*

Finish the Lesson

Why doesn't sin lead to greater freedom? Sin is actually a trap. It addicts and destroys.

When you stray, how does God restore you? Through the Gospel of His Son who came to seek and save the lost.

Closing Prayer

Focus the attention of the group by reciting "What sins should we confess?" responsively (*LSCE*, p. 24). Then pray this or a similar prayer based on the definition of confession:

Merciful Savior, sometimes after I confess my sins I still feel guilty. Through my pastor and the mutual encouragement of other Christians, grant me Your forgiveness. For you live and reign with the Father and the Holy Spirit. Amen.

Lesson Suggestions

Hymn: *LW* 230:3-5; *TLH* 329; *AGPS* 266

Homework: Read "A Short Form of Confession," *LSCE,* pages 218–219. Use the Ten Commandments to create a list of your sins. Carry the list with you to private confession with your pastor or to Sunday worship. After the service, tear up the list and throw it away.

Memory Work: Have students catch up or work ahead on memory work.

32

Office of the Keys

Focus on the Catechism

Focus the attention of the group by reciting the Office of the Keys responsively (*LSCE*, p. 27). Then pray this or a similar prayer based on the Office of the Keys:

Merciful Savior, our sin and rebellion shut us out of the kingdom of heaven and lock us into lives of self-destruction. Open heaven for us by Your forgiveness that we might enter Your presence with joy; for You live and reign with the Father and the Holy Spirit, one God now and forever. Amen.

Activity

Materials: Small suitcase with a working lock and key, filled with enough candy for all students

Say, **I have a suitcase here filled with a surprise for each person in the class. I need a volunteer to open it.** Let a volunteer attempt to open the suitcase. After a few attempts, ask why the suitcase has not yet been opened. Let the volunteer explain that it is locked. Ask, **Since the suitcase is locked, are there any suggestions for ways we might get into the suitcase?** Let the students offer suggestions. Help the students see that there are good options and poor options for getting into the suitcase. It would be possible to break into the suitcase, but then it would be ruined. You could break the lock, but then it would be ruined. You could just leave it and forget the surprise.

Somebody will suggest using a key. Say, **It makes sense that the easiest way into the suitcase is by using the key. I have the key right here. However, before we open the suitcase, let's think about how this reminds us of the Office of the Keys in the church.**

God has given the church the authority to forgive the sins of those who repent. Ask, **So how will you get this key from me?** You will want the volunteer to ask for the key. Say, **Once you asked for the key, I gave it to you freely. Now you can open the suitcase. Forgiveness is freely given by Jesus through the church to anyone who asks.**

Table Talk

(Don't just read—TELL the following true story.)

Doubt plagued Martin Luther's soul. He wanted to be sure that he would enter God's kingdom, that he would escape hell and live forever in heaven. He prayed seven times each day. He recited all 150 psalms every week, sometimes every day! He beat his body and labored until he was too sick to move. But no matter how much Luther did, he always wondered whether he had done enough, whether he was righteous enough to enter God's kingdom.

Then Luther began to study St. Paul's letter to the Romans. At first this portion of Scripture did not comfort him. He could not understand it, because for years he had been taught that he must be righteous enough to enter God's kingdom. But Paul seemed to say that it is God who makes us right, that heaven is God's gift to us in Christ. Later Luther wrote, "See, this is what is meant by 'Thy kingdom come.' You do not seek Him; He seeks you. For you do not find Him; He finds you." When Luther understood that God wants to forgive us freely through Christ, it completely changed his life.

Discuss one-on-one or in small groups the following questions. (Mentors will guide students through the lesson sheets.)

➡ Student material starts here.

Is there anything you can do to pay for your own sins and gain peace with God? Explain your answer.

No. Like Luther, you can never be sure that your own efforts are enough. Even as you do good things, you continue to do evil.

According to St. Paul's letter to the Romans, who declares us righteous and worthy of the kingdom of heaven?

God declares us righteous through Jesus Christ, our Savior.

How is the example of Luther encouraging to you?

Answers will vary. The students should note the comfort that forgiveness through Christ brought Martin Luther.

Bible Study

After an argument with the Pharisees and Saducees, Jesus warns His disciples about the Pharisees' teachings. He then asks His disciples a life-changing question. Read Matthew 16:13–19.

1. According to Jesus (vv. 17–19), what serves as the foundation of the church?

Jesus Christ is the foundation of the church. It is upon His life, death, and resurrection that all our faith depends and trusts. Without Him we have no hope.

2. What opens the kingdom of heaven?

The keys of the kingdom—God's Word of forgiveness through Baptism, Absolution, and the Lord's Supper.

3. What closes the kingdom of heaven?

Our sins and unrepentance.

4. Who has been given the authority to forgive sins or to withhold forgiveness?

God gives this authority to His church. Pastors exercise this authority or "Office of the Keys" publicly. However, every Christian can share the message of God's forgiveness.

5. At Sunday morning Divine Service, whom has the church "called" to exercise this authority?

The students should name their called pastor(s).

6. Share a time in your life when you felt especially joyful and thankful for the forgiveness God offered you.

Answers will vary.

7. Does everyone who speaks words of confession automatically get forgiven? Who does not receive forgiveness? Why not?

No. People who simply pretend to be sorry do not receive forgiveness because they are insincere. They fight against the Holy Spirit's work in their lives.

8. Point out how the Bible story proclaims the Law and the Gospel.

For example, 16:17–18 proclaims that the heavenly Father gives us His kingdom and not even hell can overcome it. In 16:19 Christ tells the apostles they have authority to bind the sins of the impenitent as long as they do not repent (Law) as well as the authority to loose the sins of those who repent (Gospel).

Family in Faith Journal

Have students describe a time when they were locked out (e.g., from their home or a car). Did the experience change the way they did things in the future? Who had the key? How is this like the Office of the Keys? Parents/mentors should record the story in the Family in Faith Journal.

Fun for Review

Props: Several keys strung together

Characters: Jenny, Marlys, Stu (who has a large collection of keys hanging from his belt loop)

Setting: Anywhere

JENNY: What's up with all the keys, Stu?

MARLYS: You look like the school janitor.

STU: I've started collecting them.

JENNY: Do you have to hang your collection from your pants?

MARLYS: It looks kind of weird.

STU: I think it looks cool.

JENNY: Are you trying to make a fashion statement or something?

STU: No, I just want to be prepared.

MARLYS: For what? Hoping to be named honorary locksmith of the week?

JENNY: Hoping the President of the United States will name you to a *key* cabinet position?

STU: No! It's bigger than that!

JENNY: Let's see, *key*note speaker at the United Nations? Or janitor to the Ambassadors' Club?

MARLYS: I give up.

STU: You guys think you're so smart. You'll see. I'm collecting keys to the kingdom.

JENNY: What kingdom?

STU: The kingdom of God.

MARLYS: You've lost your mind, Stu. Keys for the kingdom of God? You mean … heaven?

STU: Yep.

JENNY: And do you think one of those keys you have is going to get you into heaven?

STU: I'm not sure about that.

MARLYS: What a minute. Does this have to do with the Office of the Keys that Pastor Jon was talking about last week?

STU: That's the one.

JENNY: You're a little mixed up, my friend.

MARLYS: I'll say!

STU: But we were talking about what Peter said when Jesus asked him, "Who do people say that I am?"

JENNY: And Peter said that although the people gave different answers, He knew He was the Christ, the Son of the living God.

STU: Then it says that Jesus gave him the "keys of the kingdom of heaven." When I die, I want to make sure I have the keys to the kingdom.

JENNY: I think the *key* to this conversation is that you are confused, Stu!

MARLYS: The key to the kingdom isn't made of metal or whatever keys are made of.

JENNY: The key to getting into the kingdom of heaven is knowing Jesus in a personal way.

MARLYS: It's about having His forgiveness through Baptism, His Word, and the Lord's Supper.

JENNY: It's about having faith in Jesus.

STU: So having God's forgiveness through Jesus and confessing Him as my Savior opens heaven for me?

JENNY: You've got it!

STU: So without realizing it, I've had the key to heaven all along—ever since the Holy Spirit created faith in me at my Baptism.

MARLYS: I think he's figured it out!

STU: First thing I'm doing is getting rid of all these keys hanging from my belt loop. They were pulling my pants down anyway!

Finish the Lesson

What opens God's kingdom for us? God opens His kingdom to us through the forgiveness of sins in the Word and Sacraments.

What closes God's kingdom for us? Our sin and unrepentance close God's kingdom to us. When someone refuses to repent, the pastor may tell them that heaven is closed to them.

Closing Prayer

Focus the attention of the group by reciting the Office of the Keys responsively (*LSCE*, p. 27). Then pray this or a similar prayer based on the Office of the Keys:

Merciful Savior, our sin and rebellion shut us out of the kingdom of heaven and lock us into lives of self-destruction. Open heaven for us by Your forgiveness that we might enter Your presence with joy; for You live and reign with the Father and the Holy Spirit, one God now and forever. Amen.

Lesson Suggestions

Hymn: *LW* 235; *TLH* 331; *AGPS* 88

Homework: *LSCE* questions 269–284. Have students write a summary paragraph of what they learned or answer the questions in *Exploring Luther's Small Catechism,* pages 57E–58G.

Memory Work: The Office of the Keys; Matthew 16:19 (895); Galatians 6:1-2 (914)

Prayer upon Completing Study of **Confession and Absolution**

Following the sermon, the confirmands and their parents/mentors shall come forward. They shall face the congregation, confirmands in front, parents/mentors behind. Then the minister shall say:

Beloved in the Lord, on the night that Jesus rose from the dead, He visited the disciples in the Upper Room and called them to forgive sins.

The students shall then speak together the words of confession.

Let us pray for our catechumens, that our Lord God would open their hearts and the door of His mercy that they may remain faithful to Christ Jesus, our Lord:

Almighty God and Father, because You always grant growth to Your Church, increase the faith and understanding of our catechumens that, recalling the new birth by the water of Holy Baptism, they may forever continue in the family of those whom You adopt as Your sons and daughters; through Jesus Christ, our Lord.

Response: Amen.

Adapted from *Lutheran Worship*, pp. 205, 276

Sacrament of the Altar

Focus on the Catechism

Focus the attention of the group by reciting the definition of the Sacrament of the Altar responsively (*LSCE,* pp. 28–29). Then pray this or a similar prayer based on the Sacrament of the Altar:

Lord Jesus Christ, You instituted this holy meal and invited us to attend. Teach us to draw near to Your table in all humility. Quench our spiritual thirst with Your very life blood. Feed us with Your true body, for You live and reign with the Father and the Holy Spirit, one God now and forever. Amen.

Activity

Materials: Pre-measured ingredients for chocolate chip cookies, spoons

Have students mix ingredients thoroughly. Give spoons to the students, and ask them to find the eggs in the dough. They will quickly realize that this is impossible. Ask, **Why?** (Because the eggs are completely mixed in.) **Are they really present?** (Yes. They are mixed into the dough so thoroughly they can't be seen.)

Say, **In the catechism, Luther tells us that Jesus' body and blood are really present in, with, and under the bread and wine of the Lord's Supper. Just as we can't see the eggs in this cookie dough, we can't see the body and blood of Christ in the Lord's Supper. Yet we know from Jesus' promise that they are there for our benefit.**

If possible, have a volunteer bake the cookies to eat later.

Table Talk

(Don't just read—TELL the following true story.)

Members of the Church of Our Lady in Halle, Germany, have told us a remarkable story from the end of Martin Luther's life. While serving Holy Communion, Luther's arms grew weary because so many people came for the Sacrament. His hands began to tremble, and he accidentally spilled some of the Communion wine on the floor. But instead of ignoring the spilled wine or leaving it for someone to step in, Luther placed the chalice on the altar, got down on his hands and knees, and drank up the spilled wine! When the congregation saw what Luther had done, they were amazed and broke into tears.

Discuss one-on-one or in small groups the following questions. (Mentors will guide students through the lesson sheets.)

➡ Student material starts here.

Why would Luther drink up the spilled Communion wine?

This wine had been consecrated or set aside for the Lord's Supper so God's people could receive the blood of Christ.

Why might the congregation break into tears over this?

By this action, Luther showed how deeply he respected God's Sacrament. He treasured the elements of the Lord's Supper so that everyone would know how sacred it was.

How seriously did the early Lutherans take the Lord's Supper?

Very!

Bible Study

The leaders of Judah plot to take Jesus' life. Judas—one of Jesus' disciples—arranges for Jesus' arrest. Knowing all of this, Jesus focuses on having one last meal with the disciples before His death. Read Matthew 26:17–30.

1. What did Jesus know would happen to Him soon? See verse 21.

Jesus would soon be betrayed by one of His own disciples, Judas.

2. Even with that knowledge, what did Jesus do with the disciples?

He communed with them; He had fellowship.

3. Contrast Jesus' actions with our own when we've been betrayed or hurt by a friend. Afterward do we want to talk with the friend, much less eat with him or her? In what way is Holy Communion a meal of oneness for us on Sunday morning, despite our differences?

It is a meal of oneness because we come together in one faith confessing Jesus Christ.

4. What does Jesus announce He's giving through this Supper? See verses 26–28.

His own true body and blood.

5. Read 1 Corinthians 10:16. Besides bread and wine, what else is received according to St. Paul?

Jesus' body and blood.

6. The Bible in no way suggests that the body and blood are only there symbolically. So why do you think some churches feel compelled to teach only a symbolic presence in the Supper?

They teach a symbolic presence because they say that, humanly speaking, it is impossible to eat Jesus' body and blood since they are in heaven. They fail to realize that in a supernatural, sacramental way it is indeed possible and does happen.

7. Explain in your own words why Holy Communion is so important for considering that Jesus comes in, with, and under the bread and wine with His very presence.

Answers will vary.

8. Recall a special victory celebration, such as after your team has won the area soccer tournament. How is the Lord's Supper an even greater celebration of victory?

We celebrate Christ's victory over sin, death, and the power of the devil.

9. Point out where the Bible passage proclaims the Law and the Gospel.

For example, Matthew 26:21–25 condemns Judas for betraying Jesus. Matthew 26:27–28 promises us the forgiveness of sins through the Lord's Supper.

Family in Faith Journal

Students should ask their parent or mentor to explain what it means for him/her to attend Holy Communion. Students should record the answer in the Family in Faith Journal.

Fun for Review

Props: Bible, notebook paper and pencil, notepad and pen, calculator

Characters: Bobby, Suzy, Amy, Narrator, Billy

Setting: A classroom with a desk or two

(BOBBY is working with a calculator, pencil, and notebook paper.)

SUZY: *(Enters with AMY)* What are you doing?

BOBBY: Excuse me, Sooz, I'm busy.

SUZY: I say, Sir William, this is STUDY HALL! You shouldn't be working so hard.

BOBBY: I'm trying to come up with a formula that proves Christ is truly present in the Lord's Supper. That way Billy can't argue about things like he usually does.

AMY: What?

BOBBY: I think I can prove that Christ's body and blood are truly present in the bread and wine.

AMY: And how long have you been working on this *formula*?

BOBBY: A while. Now, if you don't mind!

SUZY: I have an idea that might help you, little Luther.

BOBBY: *(Perking up)* You do?

SUZY: Sure. Ask the pastor if you can have one of those pieces of bread. Get a microscope from the lab and, get this—look at it!

BOBBY: Hmmmm.

AMY: Both of you—that's ridiculous! That's not how you do it. You don't need a microscope or a calculator, you need a Bible! Have you considered the Bible in your formula, Bobby?

BOBBY: Yeah, but that doesn't actually prove that Christ is really present in this Sacrament. It just says that He is.

AMY: And you have a problem with that?

BOBBY: No, I don't. But what about Billy? He probably thinks it's just an exaggeration or something. If I could just point him to a formula or something that proves it.

(AMY gets a Bible.)

AMY: How about pointing him to this from the Gospel of Matthew: "While they were eating, Jesus took bread, gave thanks and broke it, and gave it to His disciples, saying, 'Take and eat; this is My body.' Then He took the cup, gave thanks and offered it to them, saying, 'Drink from it, all of you. This is My blood.'"

BOBBY: I thought of that. But then Billy will say, "Yeah, but Jesus also says that He is the vine and we are the branches." Then he'll say, "Does that mean every grapevine is actually Jesus?"

AMY: Of course not. Remind him that we interpret God's Word by taking into account the other Scripture passages around it. And nowhere does it say you can sin against a grapevine. But it does say you can sin against the body and blood of Jesus if you take the Lord's Supper in an unworthy manner.

BOBBY: Like not believing that Christ is really present or doubting His Word! See my problem?

NARRATOR: The next morning, before confirmation class …

(BOBBY, AMY, and SUZY approach BILLY, who is about to go into class. He looks suspiciously at the three. They look determined.)

AMY: We have a question or two to ask you, Billy.

BILLY: What?

BOBBY: *(Pulling out a notepad and pen like a detective ready to take notes)* How do you feel about the Lord's Supper?

BILLY: I can't wait for First Communion. And no wisecracks! I'm really looking forward to taking the Lord's Supper. *(Looking at BOBBY's notepad)* What are you doing?

BOBBY: Do you really believe that Jesus is present in the Lord's Supper?

BOBBY: Of course!

AMY and SUZY: YOU DO?

BOBBY: *(A little antagonistic)* How do you know for sure?

BILLY: It's called faith, Bobby-boy!

SUZY: *(Ripping the notepad and pen away from BOBBY and playing detective)* Yeah, but how can you be certain you're not just receiving something that represents the body and blood of Christ?

BILLY: Because Jesus said, "This IS My body" and "This IS My blood." Jesus created the world, was born of a virgin, and rose from the dead. Why should I doubt His Word in the Lord's Supper?

SUZY: There's your formula, Sir Robert. God's promise yields *faith*.

149

Finish the Lesson

If someone asked you why you believe Christ is present in the Lord's Supper, how would you respond? Christ, the Maker of heaven and earth, the worker of miracles, has promised.

Where does faith come from? The Holy Spirit creates faith in our hearts through the Word and Sacraments.

Closing Prayer

Focus the attention of the group by reciting the definition of the Sacrament of the Altar responsively (*LSCE*, pp. 28–29). Then pray this or a similar prayer based on the Sacrament of the Altar:

Lord Jesus Christ, You instituted this holy meal and invited us to attend. Teach us to draw near to Your table in all humility. Quench our spiritual thirst with Your very life blood. Feed us with Your true body, for You live and reign with the Father and the Holy Spirit, one God now and forever. Amen.

Lesson Suggestions

Hymn: *LW* 238; *TLH* 313; *AGPS* 66

Homework: *LSCE* questions 285–295. Have students write a summary paragraph of what they learned or answer the questions in *Exploring Luther's Small Catechism*, pages 59–60.

Memory Work: "The Nature of the Sacrament of the Altar" (*LSCE*, pp. 227–28); 1 Corinthians 10:16 (926); John 15:5 (944)

34

Benefits of the Sacrament of the Altar

Focus on the Catechism

Focus the attention of the group by reciting the benefits of the Sacrament of the Altar responsively (*LSCE,* p. 29). Then pray this or a similar prayer based on the benefits of the Sacrament:

Dearest Jesus, we hunger, thirst, and depend on Your blessings. Teach us to love Your Sacrament and receive it often; for You live and reign with the Father and the Spirit, forever and ever. Amen.

Activity

Materials: Variety of food and beverage items, Communion chalice and wafers

Have examples of various food and drink on the table. Ask, **What are the benefits of these different foods?** Allow students to answer. Remove the food. Then ask, **How long could you live without food?** (A few weeks.) Ask about the value of the different drinks on the table. Say, **How long could you live without something to drink?** (No more than three days.)

Put the Communion chalice and wafers on the table. Say, **When Jesus gave the Lord's Supper to His disciples, He told them to eat it and drink it until He returned.** Ask, **Based on the catechism, what are the benefits of the Lord's Supper?** (Forgiveness of sins, life, and salvation.) **Should you try to live without them by staying away from the Lord's Table?** (No. The Lord's Supper is a special privilege and blessing. God's people should receive it often.)

Table Talk

(Don't just read—TELL the following true story.)

On April 25, 1525, a crowd flooded the Minster church in Zurich, Switzerland. The people did not gather to witness some new spectacle. They gathered because something precious, something they treasured, was being taken from them. The rulers of Zurich had decided to change the celebration of the Lord's Supper. The people had this one last opportunity to receive Christ's body and blood in their city.

The man behind the changes was Ulrich Zwingli. Zwingli did not believe that Jesus could give us His body and blood in the Lord's Supper. So he rewrote the worship service, removing this promise of Christ.

Remarkably, on the night that Zwingli betrayed the Lord's Supper, he had a disturbing dream. He dreamt that he was debating about the Lord's Supper with one of the city officials who still believed in Christ's promise. In his dream Zwingli felt like his tongue was paralyzed. He could not debate. But then a mysterious being appeared to him and told him how to preach that Christ was not truly present in the Lord's Supper.

Discuss one-on-one or in small groups the following questions. (Mentors will guide students through the lesson sheets.)

➡ Student material starts here.

Why did the people of Zurich flock to church in 1525?

They realized that they would soon lose the privilege of receiving Christ's body and blood in the Lord's Supper.

Why did Zwingli rewrite the worship service?

He did not believe the promise of Christ.

Discuss Zwingli's dream. Which is more reliable: dreams or the teachings of the Bible?

Zwingli should have trusted the Word of Christ rather than depend on a dream. His actions have affected the lives of thousands of people, since many churches have made Zwingli's doctrine their official teaching.

Bible Study

God gives the apostle John visions of the end of the world and the glory of heaven. Read Revelation 19:4–9

1. How does John describe heaven?

John describes heaven as a great wedding banquet. Heaven is a party!

2. Who attends this heavenly party?

Angels and those made righteous through the blood of Christ.

3. Where do the righteous acts of the saints come from? See verse 8.

God gives them to us. They are part of His blessing for us.

4. If in the Lord's Supper we celebrate the real presence of Christ's body and blood, what will we celebrate in heaven someday? See verse 9.

We will celebrate at the great banquet feast with God and in the company of all His people. We celebrate Christ's victory.

5. Read Matthew 26:29. What promise about heaven does Jesus connect with the Lord's Supper?

He will drink it anew with us in heaven.

6. If worship centers around the Lord's Supper in heaven, what should our worship here on earth center around?

The Lord's Supper.

7. If the Lord's Supper is so wonderful, why not fly a plane over all the large cities of the world and simply drop the Lord's Supper in little packets so that everyone receives the blessings?

One can only receive these blessings through faith in Jesus Christ.

8. Point out where the passage proclaims the Law and the Gospel.

For example, 19:10 rebukes those who worship anything other than God. In Revelation 19:7–8 God's people celebrate the gifts of righteousness and eternal life given through Christ, the Lamb of God.

Family in Faith Journal

Parents/mentors should describe why they go to Communion and how they prepare. Have students record these thoughts in the Family in Faith Journal.

Fun for Review

Characters: Mrs. Bunt, Shawn

Setting: Bakery

SHAWN: Hi, Mrs. Bunt. I saw your "Help Wanted" sign in the bakery window. I'm here because I need a job.

MRS. BUNT: Hi, Shawn! It's a treat to see you two days in a row—at church yesterday and now you're here for a job. Why do you need a job?

SHAWN: I need some spending money because my parents don't give me enough allowance.

MRS. BUNT: And what do you need to spend this money on?

SHAWN: I need to buy cool clothes. I need money to pay for junk food when I go out with my friends. I need money to spend on stuff when we go on vacation this summer.

MRS. BUNT: Sounds like you are in desperate need, Shawn.

SHAWN: You don't need to tell me that! So what's the job you have open?

MRS. BUNT: I need a kneader.

SHAWN: You need a kneader?

MRS. BUNT: I need someone to come in and knead the dough for the breads we make. To make the bread rise, we add yeast and then someone needs to knead the dough. Then we let it sit for a while before we knead the dough again. The dough needs to be kneaded several times before we bake it.

SHAWN: Well, I need a job and you need a kneader. Can we work something out?

MRS. BUNT: Can you start tomorrow?

SHAWN: Do you need me to knead tomorrow? I have a big paper I need to write for confirmation class.

MRS. BUNT: Well, that's important. I guess I don't *need* for you to start tomorrow. What are you supposed to write about for class?

SHAWN: We're studying the Lord's Supper. My assignment is to write about my need for forgiveness, life, and salvation.

MRS. BUNT: I *know* I need that.

SHAWN: Me too, Mrs. Bunt.

MRS. BUNT: You've been telling me this afternoon about what you need. You said you need a job; you need money for junk and stuff; you need spending money.

SHAWN: And you need a kneader! Soon I'll be a professional kneader!

MRS. BUNT: But I'd say that most of those things you mentioned are things you want, not necessarily *need*. There is a difference.

SHAWN: Good point. Maybe that's what I'll write about—the difference between things we want and things we need.

MRS. BUNT: And we need the Lord's Supper most of all. Unfortunately, not everyone realizes that.

SHAWN: I definitely need God's forgiveness and the gift of life in heaven.

MRS. BUNT: That's for sure.

SHAWN: Mrs. Bunt, I think I'll be able to start work for you tomorrow after all. After talking to you, I think I've just about got this paper written.

MRS. BUNT: That would be great, Shawn. You know why?

SHAWN: Because you need a kneader?

MRS. BUNT: That's right. And now you need to get home. And write that report about what we both really need most!

Finish the Lesson

What do we need most of all? Forgiveness through Christ.

How often does a Christian need the Lord's Supper? The Bible never specifically says how often we should take the Lord's Supper. However, we certainly sin often and need God's forgiveness. The early Christians and Lutheran Reformers celebrated the Lord's Supper weekly.

Closing Prayer

Focus the attention of the group by reciting the benefits of the Sacrament of the Altar responsively (*LSCE,* p. 29). Then pray this or a similar prayer based on the benefits of the Sacrament:

Dearest Jesus, we hunger, thirst, and depend on Your blessings. Teach us to love Your Sacrament and receive it often; for You live and reign with the Father and the Spirit, forever and ever. Amen.

Lesson Suggestions

Hymn: *LW* 240; *TLH* 307; *AGPS* 82

Homework: *LSCE* questions 296–298. Have students write a summary paragraph of what they learned or answer the questions in *Exploring Luther's Small Catechism,* pages 60A–61C.

Memory Work: "The Benefit of the Sacrament of the Altar" (*LSCE,* p. 233); "The Power of the Sacrament of the Altar" (*LSCE,* p. 236); Matthew 26:28 (945); 1 Corinthians 10:17 (953)

STOP!

Everyone knows that the greatest dilemma in confirmation is that students fall away after they have finished studying the catechism. Take a proactive step. Have parents/mentors get out their calendars and set a date for a confirmation retreat six months to a year from now. The purpose of this retreat will be to renew the confirmands in their vows. For ideas on how to organize your retreat, turn to page 160 at the back of this guide.

35

Worthy Reception

Focus on the Catechism

Focus the attention of the group by reciting "Who receives this sacrament worthily?" responsively (*LSCE*, p. 29). Then pray this or a similar prayer based on the worthy reception of the Sacrament:

Lord, You created heaven and earth by Your Word. You healed the sick and raised the dead with a touch of Your hand. Grant us faith and faithfulness to believe Your promise of forgiveness and to feed at Your table often; in Your name we pray. Amen.

Activity

Materials: Warm coat, gloves, rope, sleeping bag, backpack, other hiking or mountain gear that is easily accessible

Ask for two volunteers. Have the volunteers come to the front of the class. Give all the hiking gear and warm clothing to one of the volunteers. Have that volunteer dress for a hike. Let the other volunteer stand there in regular clothing. Now set up the situation by saying the following. **You have just paid for a mountain-hiking expedition. The company organizing the trip is giving you your choice of guides.** Point to the two. **The mountain you're climbing has snow on the top. It also has steep cliffs. It will take you several days to get to the top. One guide will only take what you see he/she has right now.** Point to the volunteer without any gear. **The other guide is also ready to go right now. Which guide appears worthy of your trust for this mountain expedition?** Ask the class the reasons for their decision. Most of the class will probably choose the guide that has the equipment needed for the trip. Point out that one guide looks ready and knowledgeable for the trip while the other guide looks unworthy and unprepared.

Say, **We are taught that anyone who has faith and trust in Jesus' words, "given and shed for you for the forgiveness of sins," is worthy and well prepared to receive Holy Communion. On our own we would be like the first guide, unprepared for the journey of faith and to celebrate Holy Communion. However, God prepares our hearts so that we believe that the forgiveness offered in Communion benefits us.**

Table Talk

(Don't just read—TELL the following true story.)

The "Christian Questions with Their Answers" section has long appeared in editions of Luther's Small Catechism. For centuries people assumed that Luther wrote them. But historians have recently discovered that they were first published three years after Luther's death. They are probably the work of Dr. Johann Lang, a close personal friend of Luther who had lived with him in the Augustinian monastery and supported him throughout the Reformation. The questions and answers help us understand how to prepare for receiving the Lord's Supper.

Read "Christian Questions with Their Answers" responsively.

Discuss one-on-one or in small groups the following questions. (Mentors will guide students through the lesson sheets.)

➡ Student material starts here.

What teachings of the Bible do "Christian Questions with Their Answers" emphasize?

That we are sinners, the person of Christ, the Holy Trinity, the real presence of Christ in the Sacrament, and so on.

Why are these important for the Lord's Supper?

Christ did not institute the Lord's Supper for the immature and ignorant. For example, He gave the Lord's Supper to His disciples after He had taught them His Word.

In view of these questions, should just anyone receive the Lord's Supper?

No. In this lesson we will learn about self-examination as taught by the apostle Paul in 1 Corinthians 11.

Bible Study

The congregation in Corinth is deeply troubled and divided. While instructing them about worship, Paul turns to the topic of the Lord's Supper. He reviews many basic teachings with them that they have studied with him before. Read 1 Corinthians 11:17–34.

1. What kind of objection did St. Paul have with the way the Corinthians partook of Holy Communion? See verses 17–22.

They were eating and drinking the Lord's Supper like a dinner meal, to the extent that they were even getting drunk on the wine.

2. What kind of examination does Paul recommend we do before partaking of the Lord's Supper?

St. Paul reminds us that we are to examine ourselves to see if we are penitent and if we recognize Jesus' real presence in the Sacrament.

3. Why do we have to examine ourselves when we're already Christians?

Christians, like all people, continue to sin and need to repent. We certainly do not want to take Holy Communion to our harm.

4. Think back on a past lesson regarding the "real presence" of Christ in the Sacrament. What does the phrase "without recognizing the body of the Lord" mean (v. 29)?

Jesus is truly present in, with, and under the bread.

5. What joy comes from knowing that one actually receives His real presence in the Lord's Supper?

There is great joy in knowing that Jesus' very presence is coming to us, the Jesus who gave His body on the cross for us, the Jesus who shed His blood on the cross for us. His very presence comes to us through this Sacrament.

6. What does verse 26 suggest regarding the frequency of taking Holy Communion?

That we partake of it often.

7. Point out where the Bible passage proclaims the Law and the Gospel.

For example, 1 Corinthians 11:17–22 rebukes the Corinthians for abusing the Lord's Supper. 1 Corinthians 11:23–26 points them back to Jesus' words of blessing in the Lord's Supper.

Family in Faith Journal

Have students describe a time they felt unworthy of love or friendship. Listen and discretely record the experience in the Family in Faith Journal. Also offer them encouragement through Christ.

Fun for Review

Characters: Usher, Person 1, Person 2, Person 3 (a male), Person 4 (a male), Person 5

Setting: People are in a line, ready to approach the Lord's Table. After each person's thoughts are vocalized, the USHER motions to let the person go forward to the Table. The person exits out of view.

(PERSON 1 is checking a watch.)

PERSON 1: Well, look at the time. Boy, is this service long! Maybe I'll leave right after I take Communion. I don't have time to stick around for more singing and prayers and whatever. Well, looks like it's my turn. *(Starting to walk forward)* Now, let's see, what was I supposed to do? Oh yeah, I need to pick up milk on the way home from church today. *(USHER motions PERSON 1 forward.)*

PERSON 2: Look at these people taking Communion. They don't deserve it! Who's that person? I've never seen her before. She's probably not even Lutheran—probably a guest that didn't see our Communion policy. Poor lady—I hope the pastor passes her over. This is for us, lady! She doesn't even realize what she's taking. Oh, I'd like to talk to her. Hey! How come that usher didn't stop her from going up to Communion? There she goes, eating and drinking to her own condemnation! *(USHER motions PERSON 2 forward.)*

PERSON 3: Thank You, Lord, once again, for this opportunity to be strengthened in my faith toward You. I don't deserve the forgiveness I am ready to receive, but I know it's there because of Your love. I pray that this meal would also strengthen me, first to be a better husband, and from there a better father, and from there a better servant in Your kingdom. Amen. *(USHER motions PERSON 3 forward.)*

PERSON 4: I have so much hate in my heart for what she did to me! Forgive her? You have to be kidding me! Good thing I'm going to get forgiveness. *(Looking around)* In fact, I don't think she's even here this morning. Good! I don't want to even see her face! Of course, in a way I hope she is here. Yeah! Then she can see me standing up here, doing just fine. Lookin' good! That's right. Look at me. I'm okay … you little … *(Mumbles under breath)* *(USHER motions PERSON 4 forward.)*

PERSON 5: It's been a while, Lord. You know, I really shouldn't be taking Communion. I haven't forgotten that I'm actually receiving the true body and blood of Jesus Christ—"in, with, and under the bread and wine." I remember that from my confirmation years. But it's been so long since I've been in church. I've done so much to shame You, Lord. I've brought so much shame on myself. You know, Lord, the pastor visited me and asked me to come back. I said I would, and here I am. But should I be here?

Finish the Lesson

What should you focus on before taking the Lord's Supper? Our need for forgiveness through Christ and the fact that He is truly present to grant us this blessing.

If you have doubts about taking the Lord's Supper, what should you do? Turn to God's Word for encouragement. Speak with your pastor or a Christian friend who can guide you from God's Word.

Closing Prayer

Focus the attention of the group by reciting "Who receives this sacrament worthily?" responsively (*LSCE,* p. 29). Then pray this or a similar prayer based on the worthy reception of the Sacrament:

Lord, You created heaven and earth by Your Word. You healed the sick and raised the dead with a touch of Your hand. Grant us faith and faithfulness to believe Your promise of forgiveness and to feed at Your table often; in Your name we pray. Amen.

Lesson Suggestions

Hymn: *LW* 239; *TLH* 305; *AGPS* 154

Homework: *LSCE* questions 299–306. Have students write a summary paragraph of what they learned or answer the questions in *Exploring Luther's Small Catechism,* page 61, D–E.

Memory Work: "Who receives this sacrament worthily?" (*LSCE*, p. 238)

Prayer upon Completing Study of the Lord's Supper

Following the sermon, the confirmands and their parents/mentors shall come forward. They shall face the congregation, confirmands in front, parents/mentors behind. Then the minister shall say:

Beloved in the Lord, on the same night on which He was betrayed, Jesus gathered with His disciples in an Upper Room and instituted the Lord's Supper.

The students shall then speak together the words of the Lord's Supper.

Let us pray for our catechumens, that our Lord God would open their hearts and the door of His mercy that they may remain faithful to Christ Jesus, our Lord:

Almighty God and Father, because You always grant growth to Your Church, increase the faith and understanding of our catechumens that, recalling the new birth by the water of Holy Baptism, they may forever continue in the family of those whom You adopt as Your sons and daughters; through Jesus Christ, our Lord.

Response: Amen.

Adapted from *Lutheran Worship*, pp. 205, 276

Retreat Options

The greatest dilemma in catechesis is that students fall away after they have finished studying the catechism. Even if your congregation has an active youth ministry, schedule a one-night retreat for your confirmands and their parents/mentors while they are still in class. By doing so, you will take a proactive step toward solving the problem of confirmands falling away. Here are some ideas for your retreat:

- Choose a comfortable atmosphere. Perhaps one of the families would open up their home for the event.
- Have confirmands prepare a meal for their parents/mentors as a way of saying "thank you" for all their support.
- Use entries from the Family in Faith Journals as discussion starters for devotions.
- Discuss what challenges and blessings the confirmands have experienced now that they are confirmed. Have students record their thoughts in the Family in Faith Journals (if they still have room to write).

Finish the evening with the following activity:

Materials: Candles with hand protectors for each person, matches, a copy of the confirmation vows

Have participants, with unlit candles in hand, form a circle around the room. Then turn off all the lights. The darker you can make the room, the better! Talk about how this is like life without Christ—total darkness. Then, after giving the people time to appreciate the darkness, have an assistant bring a lighted candle into the room. He/she should light your candle. Then you light the ones on either side, and those people should in turn light the next candles, and so on, until all the candles are lit. Don't hurry this exercise. As the candles are being lit, remind the students of how God comes to people—through the church as it proclaims Word and Sacrament. Note not only the growing light, but the decreasing darkness!

After all the candles are lit, your assistant should put out his/her candle and walk around the outside of the circle. The assistant should come up behind one of the confirmands and blow out his/her candle. As this happens, talk about how Satan wants to snuff out our faith. But God, through the church, rekindles that light of faith. Have someone relight the blown-out candle. (Note: Experience shows that parents will relight their child's candle without being asked!)

While you are standing in your circle of light, have students repeat their vows from their confirmation service. Close with prayer, thanking the Holy Spirit for giving them faith and for uniting His church.

Prayerfully consider scheduling a second retreat six months to a year after the first!